D1336556

On the Banks of the Dodder

The Dodder. Co. Dublin.

First published 2019 by
The O'Brien Press Ltd,
12 Terenure Road East, Rathgar, Dublin 6, D06 HD27, Ireland.
Tel: +353 1 4923333; Fax: +353 1 4922777
E-mail: books@obrien.ie; Website: www.obrien.ie
The O'Brien Press is a member of Publishing Ireland.

ISBN: 978-1-84717-133-7

Published in:

DUBLIN
UNESCO
City of Literature

6 5 4 3 2 1
23 22 21 20 19

Printed by EDELVIVES, Spain.
The paper in this book is produced using pulp from managed forests

On the Banks of the Dodder

Rathgar & Churchtown:

An Illustrated History

GED WALSH

Illustrations by Michael O'Brien

THE O'BRIEN PRESS
DUBLIN

DEDICATION

FOR DYMPS, MARK, BARRY, ANNA, ALEX AND ?.

Ged Walsh has always been interested in local history, having been a member of the Old Dublin Society since 1970 and studied for a diploma in local history with Maynooth University in 2008. He is also a member of the Rathmines, Ranelagh and Rathgar Historical Society since its foundation in 1996. He has given many talks to local societies and groups, particularly in south County Dublin. In rural Ireland, local history is passed down from generation to generation. This is different in an urban environment, due to a more fluid community. The motivating factor in writing this book was to outline the stories, incidents and people that have made the locality what is it today.

CONTENTS

FOREWORD

PETER PEARSON

As the River Dodder sweeps down from the Dublin Mountains towards the shallow sands of the bay at Ringsend, it flows through suburban Dublin, dividing such places as Rathfarnham and Terenure, Churchtown and Rathgar, Clonskeagh and Milltown. Although the river is a natural boundary, it falls between the line of old Dublin city and County, and the former postal districts. Perhaps as a result, areas like Rathgar and Churchtown have not been recorded and written about in a comprehensive way.

In this new book, Ged Walsh thoroughly explores all aspects of these adjoining areas, including their early history, industrial heritage and business stories, houses and architecture, churches and schools, residents both famous and not-so-famous, public and private transport, local traditions and much more besides. Ged has followed up every clue to the multi-faceted history of the district, tracking down interesting stories about owners of houses and describing living conditions in the nineteenth century. He chronicles early attempts to prevent flooding around the Dodder, and goes into much detail about what it was like to travel on the trams from Rathgar to the city.

Rathgar is well known as an impressive Victorian suburb of the city, with most of its architectural legacy dating from 1830 to about 1890. We are familiar with the redbrick terraces, the stone walls and the well-kept front gardens, with their cast-iron railings. But some readers may not realise just how many important Dublin business families lived here – household names such as the Bewleys of tea and coffee fame, or the Drummonds, who were very noted seed merchants in Dawson Street.

The significant industry that was once water-powered by the River Dodder is also little-known: the calico and paper mills, ironworks or the once-famous Milltown Laundry, whose tall brick chimney still stands beside the railway viaduct, over which the Luas glides today.

The story of Rathgar windmill is long forgotten, but it was once a dominant feature of the district, employed to pump water out of the local limestone quarry – now covered over by Herzog Park and a car park.

The supply of running water in the district, and the frequent lack of it, is another chapter in the story – a service that people now take for granted.

While Rathgar can be visualised as a discrete entity, it is much harder to see Churchtown in the same way, perhaps because there is no old village at its centre and because modern development has been allowed to spread random ugliness over its once-green fields. The area remained rural until relatively recent times. Also Dundrum has merged into Churchtown, so that it is hard to say where a defined area begins and ends. But Churchtown has much hidden history, with gems like the Bottle tower, and the famous Hazelbrook dairy, which originated nearby. There are also a surprising number of old houses, some of them from the eighteenth century, to be discovered here.

This book brings together many new illustrations and stories about the Rathgar and Churchtown districts, an under-explored area of much historical significance.

Illustrator's Note

Michael O'Brien

My early ambition was to be an artist. I became an environmental activist in the 1970s, when Dublin was being destroyed by neglect and poor planning. As a publisher, my earliest books included *The Irish Town: An Approach to Survival* by Patrick Shaffrey (1975) and *Hands Off Dublin* by Deirdre Kelly and Pat Langan (1976). I was an occupier of the Wood Quay Viking Dublin archaeological site.

Back then, I was using my drawings of key buildings as part of various environmental campaigns, but never thought this approach would be needed in Rathgar/Churchtown, where some of Dublin's best-cared-for historic buildings, squares, streetscapes and fine houses are located. My original idea, to create about twenty drawings for Ged Walsh's book, became a much wider undertaking, with an eventual sixty-seven drawings to help the campaign against the National Transport Authority's (NTA) plans to demolish railings, gardens and beautiful trees in Rathgar to make space for a six-lane 'bus corridor'. Mary Freehill, Dublin City Councillor, writes that 'Ireland has a parliament that continues to behave more like a super County Council', a reference to the elimination of local democracy.

Ged showed me many of the architectural gems of Rathgar & Churchtown, some hidden from view. We walked the Dodder River that joins the two areas – such a beautiful environmental asset. With his book, Ged has skilfully merged the superb streets, parks, squares, churches and great houses with history and the rich heritage of gifted and famous people who lived on both sides of the gracious, calm, meandering Dodder river. These stories are historically important and profoundly inspiring.

Thanks to all those who allowed us to reproduce historic postcards, photographs and maps from their private collections, and to many others who facilitated us in producing this fine book, including of course my friend and great historian Peter Pearson for his Foreword. Thanks also to Rathgar Residents Association, Rathgar Business Association, Dublin City Council Villages Department, and Christ Church Rathgar. And last but not least, the creative talent at O'Brien Press, in the heart of Rathgar village.

RATHGAR

An old map of the area, showing the 'New
Road' from Rathmines to Rathgar.

EARLY HISTORY

Where did the name Rathgar come from? Well a *rath* is a hill-fort or ring; there are over 700 townlands with 'rath' in their name in Ireland. Before the Vikings invaded Ireland, the main road out of Dublin was through Harold's Cross and Terenure. Rathgar was on a pathway that led from this road that is now Rathgar Avenue. So where was the rath? If there was one, it would have been on a prominent site. There is an incline from Rathmines to Rathgar, but it is hardly steep enough to have a rath at the summit. In those distant times, a lot of transport was done by water, so it's possible that a fort may have been over near the Dodder.

The *gar* causes another problem. It could be, as the great local historian Fred Dixon who lived in Rathgar suggests, derived from the Norse word 'garth' meaning garden. Another theory is that it could be from the Irish word *garbh*, meaning rough, or garraí, again meaning garden. It could also be a cut or trench, perhaps relating to the quarry that used to be on Orwell Road.

The earliest mention we have is of a farm at 'Ragorth' belonging to the community of St Mary de Hogges (Hogge deriving from *ogh*, Irish for 'virgin'), who had a priory at All Hallows in Dublin City, now the site of Trinity College. That community was established by Dermod Mac Murrough in 1146 for women over thirty years of age. When the religious houses were suppressed in 1539, Ragorth is stated to have had ninety acres of farmland and 1,537 acres of woodland. These lands were granted to James Sedgrave, who lived in Much Cabragh (now the Dominican convent in Cabra). He held the lands only for a short time, as they were passed on to the Cusacks, a County Meath family, later in the 1500s.

> " **Villata de Ragath.**
>
> " Et dicunt qđ in Villata de Ragarth in Cõm ꝑdc̃o est unũ mes̃ cũ ptiñ iiii.x acre terre ar̃. et iii acre subbosci et dumoȝ pcella posses- sionũ ꝑđ. quaȝ quãƚt acram terre ar̃ extenđ p annũ ad xiiᵈ.—iiiiˡˡ. xˢ. que Jacobus Rychards m̃cator tenet ad firm̃ p indentur̃ p ꝑmiõ annoȝ adhuc duranciũ ex dimissione nup Priorisse domus p'dicte reddendo inde p annũ liiiˢ. iiiiᵈ.

A reference in an old Latin text to 'Villata de Ragath' or 'Villata de Ragarth'.

13

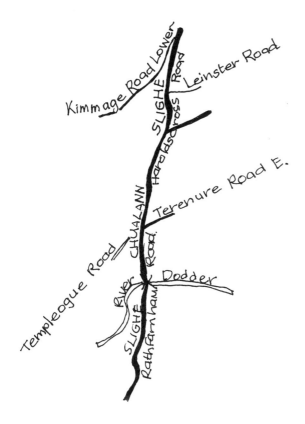

Rathfarnham Road and Harold's Cross Road follow the path of Slighe Chualann, one of the four ancient roads into Dublin.

In *History of the City of Dublin*, John T. Gilbert states that in 1570, Mr Cusack of Rathgar built over a passage near St Audoen's church in Cook Street, much to the annoyance of the locals – and more to the annoyance of St Audoen's congregation, as smoke from this building used to go into the church. Sixty-eight years later, in 1638, Robert Cusack of Rathgar was sued successfully in the ecclesiastical court, and had to remove the building.

The Reverend Nathaniel Burton relates the story of one Mrs Agnes Cusack entertaining the Earl of Essex in 1599. The Earl was served a succession of hens – roasted, boiled or spiced. When he remarked on the absence of cocks, the lady replied that hens did not associate with strange cocks when their own were away. The Earl got the hint, and did not stay the night. Rathgar ladies have always held high principles.

In 1608, John Cusack became Mayor of Dublin. He died in 1626 and is buried in St Audoen's Church. He was succeeded by Robert Cusack, who died in 1673.

During the Cromwellian invasion, and after the 1649 Battle of Rathmines, it is reported that Robert Cusack petitioned the Duke of Ormond to order his troops to stop cutting down trees and commandeering his horses. After the defeat of the Royalists, some of them took refuge for a short time in the Cusacks' house. In 1690, Nicholas Cusack lost possession of the family lands, as he was outlawed for treason. But after a few years, he resumed possession. The lands passed through the Cusack family until 1733.

John Cusack had only one heir, a daughter named Alice. Alice married John Fitzgerald of Knavinstown, County Kildare, in 1748. John was a member of the Fitzgerald family of Punchesgrange. So the lands of Rathgar came to the Fitzgeralds, and stayed in that family until 1854. Geraldine Sophia, only daughter of Charles Fitzgerald, married Alex Roper of Kent. Their son Charles, who changed his name by deed poll to Charles Roper-Fitzgerald, was called to the bar. Although owned by the Cusack and Fitzgerald family from 1850 onwards, the land was leased to different people over the years.

RATHGAR CASTLE

Up to the late eighteenth century, taxes were levied on households by a count of the number of hearths. In the hearth rolls of 1669, the House of Rathgar is given as five hearths.

Looking at the Beranger print of 1769, showing a derelict building occupied by cattle, the term 'castle' seems a bit of a misnomer. Unfortunately, it is impossible to locate the exact location of Rathgar Castle. There are several theories. The Highfield Road area is the most likely location, but which side of the road it was on is open to conjecture. One of the reasons castles were built was for the protection of the area around it. So it would be logical to have a connecting road between the castles of Rathmines and Rathgar. *Thom's Directory* of 1846 states that 'on the site of Rathgar Lodge stood Rathgar castle', showing a location that appears to be where St Luke's hospital is now.

In the 1837 Ordnance Survey map of Rathgar, 'Rathgar Castle Cottage' is located on Rathgar Avenue, perhaps lending credence to the theory that the Castle may be behind Christ Church, the Presbyterian church in the centre of Rathgar.

DEVELOPMENT

In the early 1800s, Rathgar was way out in the countryside. Dublin city at that time was stagnant, the Act of Union of 1801 having had a major effect on the economy of the city. The housing stock was decaying, and the city was burdened with a huge population of poor. It still didn't have an

Rathgar Castle, as depicted by Beranger in 1769.

adequate supply of fresh water. In 1832, it had to withstand a severe outbreak of cholera, which came to Dublin from Belfast through infected sailors. The city was poor and disease-ridden – it could truly be described as 'dirty Dublin'.

Taylor's map of 1816 shows that Rathgar was a rural spot, with few houses. Pettigrew and Oulton's *Dublin Almanac* of 1834, though not a comprehensive reference, gives nine entries for Rathgar and eleven for what is now Terenure Road East. Garville Road has twenty-nine entries. When *Thom's Directory* was first issued in 1846, the population of Rathgar is given as 745 people, living in 125 houses. In 1858, *Thom's Directory* records the population of Rathgar as 1,180, with 200 houses. Although these figures would not be totally accurate, they give a rough idea of how the area developed. By the 1850s, houses were being built in 'ribbon development', i.e. houses built singly or in terraces along main roads.

Rathgar Castle Cottage on Rathgar Road. On the right can be seen the roof of Auto Restorers car repair centre.

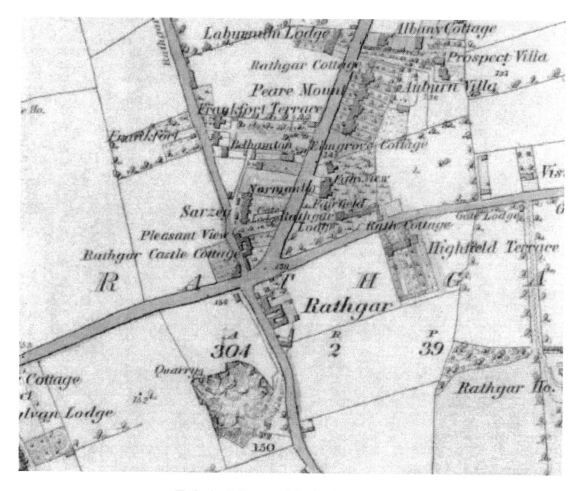

Taylor's 1816 map of the Rathgar vicinity.

This type of development started at the Rathmines end of Rathgar Road in the mid-1830s. The houses of Spireview Terrace (numbers 31 to 43) were among the first to be developed, in 1835. Houses and terraces were developed by various builders, and were named rather than numbered. The numbering of the houses didn't come till the late 1800s. They were sometimes sold, but more often let. In those days, advertisements in the papers called for the attention of all 'capitalists and developers'. Neither of these were then a derogatory term. Even in the 1840s, a lot of the houses were unoccupied due to the lack of buyers or renters. This changed with the formation of the Township of Rathmines in 1847.

The houses had some common features – a pillared main doorway, granite steps leading up to the door with a fanlight over it, and railings in front of the house and up the steps. Drainpipes were sometimes placed discreetly between houses, or more commonly at the backs of houses. Lead gullies carried the rainwater from front to rear. However, these often became blocked, causing a lot of problems. The eyesores of pipes we see today are a much later addition.

NINETEENTH-CENTURY EXPANSION – TOWNSHIP OF RATHMINES AND RATHGAR

In the 1840s, Dublin Corporation, which had become corrupt and self-serving, was reformed. The new boundaries of the city were now the Royal and Grand canals. To further this development, townships were being formed.

In 1828, a Towns Improvement Act had been passed. This provided for the establishment of townships, with boards of governors, to improve local areas. Before this time, the area of Rathgar was governed by three bodies: the Grand Jury of the City of Dublin, the Municipal Corporation

Typical beautiful Victorian homes of Rathgar Road, with wrought-iron railings and steps up to a front door with pillars and fanlight.

M.O'BRIEN © 2019

and the Grand Jury of County Dublin. Grand juries were generally composed of the landlords of an area. The Grand Jury had two functions: a judicial function, to administer justice in an area; and an administrative or fiscal function. It was responsible for roads and bridges and so on in its given area.

The roads were maintained under a tendering system, where a person would submit a price to the Grand Jury for doing a particular job. However, this led to all manner of corruption, as the tender was often submitted by a member of the Grand Jury itself. This landlord would then sub-contract the job for a lower price, and pocket the difference. Perhaps a jurist would be given a bribe to present a tender for someone else.

To free an area or a town of the Grand Jury system, an application had to be made to form a township. This was expensive, so very few such applications were made. The first place in Ireland to avail of this provision was the town of Kingstown (1821–1921), or Dún Laoghaire as it is now. The businessmen of Kingstown felt that they could prosper if they took matters in their own hands. The reason for this was the advent of the railway in Ireland; the first railway from Dublin to Kingstown was to be run from 1834.

Rathmines was also a developing area, and here again a group of businessmen decided to form their own Township. It came into being on 22 July 1847, under the chairmanship of Frederick Stokes, who lived in Belgrave House, Monkstown. The new Township had its headquarters on the site where Rathmines Town Hall now stands, the 'new' town hall being built in 1897.

If the area was to develop, a major factor in selling property was keeping rates, the levy imposed on every house or business by the local authority, low. Rathmines residents did not want to pay what they felt were the excessive rates of Dublin City. Rathmines now developed at a good pace, and space was soon running out. So in 1862, Rathgar, part of Ranelagh (Sallymount) and parts of Harold's Cross were added to the Township. This was a separate district, with three Board members. Other areas, such as Milltown, also wanted to be included, but the Board felt these areas did not have enough ratepayers, and they were rejected.

The borders of Rathmines Township were marked with boundary stones. When Rathgar joined the Township in 1862, in order to save money, the Commissioners reused the same boundary

Rathmines Town Hall, which was the headquarters of the Rathmines and Rathgar Township, then of Rathmines Urban District Council, and is now the Rathmines campus of the Dublin Institute of Technology (DIT).

The Dodder. Co. Dublin.

The weir on the Dodder, showing Carvill's sawmill.

stones, and didn't include Rathgar in the name. This is why the stones have '1847' on them. These stones are still located at the southern (Terenure) end of Terenure Road East, at Morehampton Road, at the weir on the Dodder near Orwell Bridge and also opposite the Roman Catholic Church in Harold's Cross.

Roads in the area were named with an eye on the market. The names came from the more desirable areas of England – Brighton and Grosvenor, for instance. The name Kenilworth comes from Walter Scott's novel of the name, published in 1821. Garville is a made up name – the 'Gar' is obvious, with the 'ville' added to bring a posh air to it. There was a proposal at one stage to change the name of Rathgar to Garville!

The Township structure was a good example of what we would now call Public–Private Partnership. Other townships established around this time include Blackrock (1863), Dalkey (1867) and Pembroke (Ballsbridge area, 1868).

SANITATION

Sanitation in Dublin was always a problem. It was finally taken seriously with the passing of the Public Health Act (1848). This gave power to the authorities to take action if the law was not complied with. Notices were put up ordering people to 'white wash' their houses and clear the lanes. In 1874, a more vigorous Public Health Act was passed.

In the Rathmines and Rathgar Township, the Act was not enforced too strongly. There were constant complaints to the Township, particularly in regard to the lanes at the backs of houses. Cess pits and privies caused a lot of annoyance. The flush toilet wasn't invented until 1888, and it took a few more years for it to become standard in new houses. Up to this, waste was usually dumped in cess pits in the back gardens of houses, which were emptied every so often. These cesspits were a source of contamination and pungent smells, and the sewage would seep into the ground and contaminate any stream in the area.

From the 1850s, Rathmines Township appointed Health Officers, though they were not very effective in keeping the area clean. The positions were abolished in the 1870s, as the Board felt they were not necessary. However, the Township was still very poor at enforcing proper sanitation.

In 1881, a report into the sanitation of the area was published by William Exham. It condemned the Township as being negligent in a number of aspects, and compared it very unfavourably with the Pembroke Township.

The removal of sewage from the area was undertaken in a joint operation by the Rathmines and Rathgar Township and Pembroke Township, pouring it into Dublin Bay. The infrastructure for this process was completed in 1879.

WATER SUPPLY

One big problem faced by the developing Township was the maintaining of a reliable water supply. From 1868, Dublin Corporation got its water supply from the Vartry River, under the guidance of the great Dr John Gray (1816–75), who was later knighted and whose statue by Thomas Farrell is in O'Connell Street. The city now had a pure supply of water, and the Township didn't, putting the Township under further pressure.

The Board of the Township considered that the price the Corporation wanted for supplying water was far too high. It would necessitate increasing rates in the Township, preventing people from buying or leasing houses in the area. The Board had made previous attempts to organise their own water supply, but these had proved unsuccessful.

In 1861, they arranged with the Grand Canal Company to pipe water from the canal to the Township. The reservoir was at Gallanstown, County Dublin, near the eighth lock on the Grand

The proposal for the Bohernabreena reservoir scheme, completed in 1888.

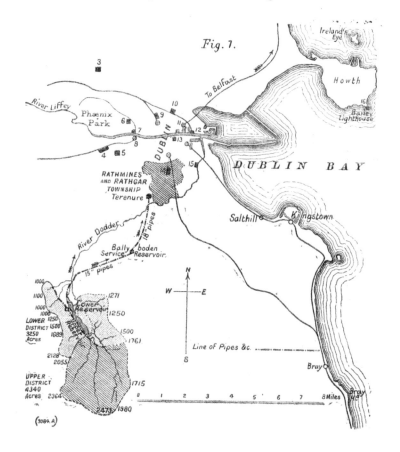

Canal. The new waterworks were officially opened by the Lord Lieutenant of Ireland, George Howard, on 23 July 1863. But Rathgar is on a height, so water pumped from the canal did not reach certain locations. The area mainly affected was from the Three Patrons Church to the southern end of the Township at Terenure Road East. To alleviate this, a pumping station was built at Harold's Cross Bridge to pump water to storage tanks. One of the main water tanks was located in the Brighton Road area, and is still indicated by the name Tower Avenue.

To facilitate the filling of the tanks, the water was turned off from midnight to 6am. But the water supply proved to be intermittent and, worse still, it was filthy. The Township assured customers that they had every confidence in a filtering system installed to purify the water. But, as this letter to the *Irish Times* states, the filtering system left a little to be desired:

The active animal you will find in the bottle I have enclosed is one of many hundreds I have found from time to time in the Rathmines water. I have drawn a tumbler full containing at least fifty of them. As I have no other to drink, and object to swallowing live bait, I am obliged to have all water intended for drinking purposes boiled and strained before using.

The matter had to be addressed.

Even before the Township had been formed in 1847, Robert Mallet (1810–81) had been approached to examine the Dodder. Dublin city commissioned him to investigate the river in regard to its flooding, but also as a possible source of water for Dublin city. Mallet issued his report in 1846. He recommended the construction of an impounding reservoir in the upper part of the Glenasmole Valley, near the ancient burial grounds of St Anne's. His report was rejected on the grounds that firstly, the quantity of water would not be adequate; secondly, to get the required quantity, an area of nine and a half square miles of bog would have to be impounded; and thirdly, the quality would be very poor.

Robert was the son of John Mallet (1780–1868), who had an iron foundry in Ryder's Row, off Capel Street. In 1847, John Mallet's home was 98 Capel Street. From 1853 to 1857, he lived at Delville House in Glasnevin, which is now the Bons Secours Hospital. Mallet's foundry manufactured the railings of Trinity College; the name 'R&J Mallet' can still be seen imprinted on them. Robert went to Trinity College, and is regarded as the world's first seismologist. As a student, he wanted to prove that energy could be transferred through sand and rock. He and his

Orwell Weir on the Dodder, designed to allow trout to swim upstream.

brother buried a barrel of explosives on Killiney Strand, and went half a mile away with a primitive seismograph to see if there was any effect. There was. I wonder would students be allowed to perform the same experiment today.

Robert was also among the first professionals to travel to see the devastation caused by the Padua earthquake in Italy in 1857. He obtained funds from the Royal Society of London through his friend, Charles Darwin. Another friend was Archibald Rowan Hamilton. Robert Mallet is regarded as one of the great engineers and geologists of the nineteenth century.

In 1877, the Township commissioners called on Richard Hassard, who had overseen the Vartry water scheme, to examine the feasibility of getting a water supply from the Dodder for the Township. Richard Hassard had the assistance of Arthur Tyrrell. Having consulted Mallet's earlier report, Hassard decided that the only way to get clean water from the bog area was to adopt what was known as a separation scheme. This had been successfully carried out at Manchester, Halifax and other places in England.

It was a huge and expensive task, including the building of the Bohernabreena reservoir. But because water had become such an important issue, the go-ahead was given. The contractors were Falkiner and Stanford of Dublin, and 700 men were employed on the project. This marvellous feat of engineering was opened on 12 March 1888, and the reservoir still supplies Rathgar's water today.

There were objectors to the scheme – the mill owners of the Dodder, who felt that their water supply would be curtailed and their mills would not work. They sued, and the case went on and on, finally landing up in the House of Lords in 1899. The Lords found in favour of the mill owners, but the decision made little difference, as by that stage new technology had replaced the waterwheel-driven mills.

SOCIAL DEVELOPMENT

From the 1860s on, Rathgar developed into a middle- and upper-class district. The residents were generally Protestant or Dissenter, and most of the houses had servants, who were Catholic. It wasn't until the 1870s that a Catholic middle class began to emerge in Ireland. A house in Rathgar would typically have a maid, who did all the chores from cooking, washing and cleaning to childminding. Some better-off households would have a cook, and in very well-to-do houses there would be several servants, including a housemaid (for general cleaning), a parlour-maid (for waiting at table), a cook and a nanny. In the larger estate houses, there would also be a gardener (sometimes more than one), as well as coachmen and stable staff.

A letter published in the *Irish Times* in the 1860s states: 'With the improved appliances of water rising in all parts of our houses and gas stoves diffusing warmth, it will soon be necessary for both fashionable and respectable people in Dublin to introduce gymnastics for the male servants and callisthenics for the female ones, to enable them to maintain their health and make a respectable appearance before company.'

In the 1880s, about eighty percent of servants were in one-servant households. These servants were generally female, and generally from the country. It was felt in the 1890s that the minimum salary required to afford a servant was £150 p.a.

Literacy levels among servants were high, and being able to read was often one of the requirements for getting a job. Employers preferred their servants to be single, and a maid's chances of meeting someone of the opposite sex were slim. Long hours and hard work left little time for social activity. The only chance a maid had of meeting anyone was when a delivery man called to the house, or after attending Mass. A servant's boyfriend was referred to as 'a follower'. When an advertisement was placed in a newspaper for a maid, it often stated 'No Followers'. If a servant got married, they were instantly dismissed from service.

In her book *Below Stairs*, Mona Hearn states that many servants were on duty from 6.30am until they retired at 10 or 11pm, well in excess of the average working day. They may have had free time at intervals during the day, but they always had to be available. Employers would say they had free time while they were going to the shops, and they wondered what servants would do with leisure time anyway. Employers often felt that a servant was lucky to have a roof over their head and to be fed. Servants generally slept in the attic, which could get very hot in summer and very cold in winter.

Half-days were introduced at the turn of the twentieth century, and servants were also entitled to two weeks' holidays. They were paid every quarter or half-year. It was a very tough life, but these positions were much sought after.

Trying to get the right servant was a major topic of conversation among ladies of that era. In her memoir *Seventy Years Young*, Lady Elizabeth Fingall states that 'countries get the Governments and people the servants they deserve'. Most ladies wanted young maids, and so unemployment among the middle-aged was a big problem. All that was left for the middle-aged maid was charring.

Local shopkeepers were the usual recruitment offices, with lists of available servants updated regularly. If a maid wanted to leave a job, she had to get a good reference from her employer. This was difficult because if she was good, the employer would want to keep her, and could refuse a reference. Sometimes, if a maid was poor or was drinking, she would get a good reference to get rid of her. Some maids were seduced by their masters. If they became pregnant, there was nothing for them. In a lot of cases, they had no choice but to enter a life of prostitution. Many ended up in the workhouse, or died by suicide.

Trade union organiser Jim Larkin, looking very dapper.

It was very difficult to get servants to organise into a union, as they worked alone. In 1909, attempts were made to start a union, but this met with a setback when, in 1911, Jim Larkin expelled women from the Irish Transport and General Workers' Union (ITGWU). He formed a separate union, the Irish Women Workers' Union, of which he was President and his sister Delia was Secretary. This union limped on, but collapsed during the 1916 Rising. It was reformed by Miss Louie Bennett in 1917. In 1918, Jim Larkin readmitted women into the ITGWU.

A great benefit to servants came in 1911 with the National Insurance Act, which would provide workers, male or female, with free medical treatment and cash if they were ill. A contribution had to be made by employers and employees, though some lady employers objected to being used as tax collectors. The Old Age Pension Act had been enacted in 1908, giving five shillings a week to people over seventy if their income from other sources did not exceed £21 p.a.

The Grand Canal at Rathmines, showing the Portobello Hotel.

29

INEXPENSIVE HOUSES
FOR SALE, WITH POSSESSION.

RATHGAR—£1,500, subject to £5 16/10. Lease 400 years.

AILESBURY ROAD—£3,000, subject only to £4 15/. Lease 160 years.

BALLSBRIDGE—£2,000, semi-detached, non-basement House, subject to £6. Lease 90 years.

LEESON PARK VICINITY — £1,400, Non-basement House, subject to £10. Lease 500 years.

SYDNEY PARADE—£1,500, subject to £4 12/9. Lease 94 years unexpired. Seen only by appointment.

SKERRIES—£1,250, Detached, on ¾ acre, subject to £3 17/6. Lease 125 years to run. Possession.

LUCAN—TO BE LET, Furnished, on moderate terms, an attractive House, with well-stocked garden. Apply to James M. North and Co., 110 Grafton street, Dublin.

DUNDRUM—DETACHED HOUSE, Furnished, 4 bedrooms, 2 sittingrooms, bathroom, servant's room, gas and gas cooker, close range, garden. Rent £15 per month, tenant keeping garden in order.

Left: A property developer's advertisement from the *Irish Times*.
Below: A bird's eye view of Rathgar village, showing O'Brien Press, Revolution pizza, Lloyd's pharmacy, the Bottler's Bank, Coman's and the 108 pubs, Donovan's butchers, Rathgar Travel, O'Brien's Wines and Boyle Sports.

The village of Rathgar as such began to develop from the 1860s. The population of the Rathmines and Rathgar Township was 20,562 in the 1871 census. To supply the growing suburb of Rathgar, grocers, butchers and fruiterers started up. Rathgar also had wine and spirit merchants, located where the two pubs are today. Rathmines was the main shopping area though, as it had more people in its catchment area. In the 1880s, there was a Coffee Palace, Refreshment and Reading rooms at 1 Orwell Road.

TRANSPORT

In 1833, Rathgar was a rural spot, far from the city of Dublin. As the area developed, people wanted easier access to the city. Omnibuses stated to appear on the streets from 1840, carrying twelve people inside and ten outside. They went from Anglesea Street to Rathfarnham, and the fare varied depending on whether you sat inside or out. In 1854, they left the terminus every half-hour, but by 1857, this was increased to every fifteen minutes. This service was not for the general populace, as a labourer earned about two shillings a day, and the fare was 4d, increasing to 6d in 1836. Rathfarnham also had an omnibus, which terminated at 5 Fownes Street. By 1845, only the Rathfarnham route was still in operation.

With the creation of the Township of Rathmines in 1847, it was decided that it needed its own transport. An omnibus service was introduced, running from Nelson's Pillar to the Rathmines office, 71 Rathmines Road. This omnibus ran at half-hourly intervals. The fare varied: initially in 1848, it was 3d; in 1850 and 1851, it was 2d; and from 1852 to 1872, it increased again to 3d. Tokens for travel were issued by the Rathmines Conveyance Association. They were engraved by William Woodhouse, and supplied by Waterhouse and Company, 25 Dame Street.

TRAMS

Even while a tram system was being planned, there was a strong effort to start a light railway line from O'Connell Street to Rathfarnham. Efforts persisted over a twelve-year period, yet, despite several promises, it never materialised.

On 1 February 1872, the first horse-drawn tram in Dublin departed from Rathgar. The terminus was at the junction of Garville Avenue and Rathgar Road, and it ran, or rather trotted, to College Green, a distance of two and a half miles. The journey took twenty minutes. This line soon extended to Terenure, and in 1876 on to Rathfarnham. The first tickets were issued by Waller of Suffolk Street.

The *Irish Times* was not impressed:

Rathgar village, complete with tram lines, in the early twentieth century.

Only a pair of horses are provided for each tram and these do not appear to be in breeding or stamina up to the mark. One omnibus was delayed for a considerable time in College Green from the horses unable to start it. When the tram is put in motion the draught is comparatively easy. A rather big tariff of three pence for a short distance is fixed and this may lead to opposition.

These trams were operated by the Dublin Tramways Company until 1 January 1881, at which point it amalgamated with the two other tramway companies operating in Dublin, to form the Dublin United Tramways Company (DUTC), under managing director William M. Murphy.

The Central Tramway Company came into being in 1876. Its terminus was College Green and it operated to Palmerston Park, Rathmines, Clonskeagh and Rathfarnham.

Mr Jas Lombard was Chairman and Mr W. Anderson, previously Manager of the Dublin Tramways Company, was Secretary. Their offices were in Sackville Street (now O'Connell Street), opposite the GPO. It was noted in an article published by the Omnibus Society that 'none of the fair sex are represented on the company's staff'.

Palmerston Park   Rathmines

The tram went past Palmerston Park.

The logistics of the operation was huge. The company had 1,000 horses, mostly animals bought within the previous three years. The average cost of buying a horse was £38.2s.6d. It ran sales every six weeks, auctioning off the 'down at heels and out at elbows animals'. The daily food allowance for a horse was 29lbs of a mixture of maize, oats and hay. Hay was imported from the Netherlands in times of scarcity. The bedding was sawdust and sand. The manure was sold off, but due to over-supply at this time, it was not a great money-maker.

Each stable kept a stock of salt for snowy conditions. Of course, no stable would be complete without a forge and a blacksmith, who, with so many horses, was never idle. A harness shop was also needed, to keep all the leathers intact.

The workshops where carriages were built and repaired for the company were located at Inchicore. This was the beginning of the 'Inchicore Works', still operated by CIÉ. Irish oak and ash, Spanish mahogany and Californian pine were all used in the construction of the carriages, which were of such high quality that they were awarded a certificate of merit at the National Exhibition of 1882. In 1884/5 the rolling stock of the country was 136 cars and three omnibuses.

Fares were initially sold in denominations of 1d, 2d and 3d, but an introduction of a fare of 1d per mile resulted in a great increase in revenue.

Of course, as well as passengers, a parcel delivery system operated all day, with the receiving offices generally being shops along each route. Each shop had a messenger boy, who would deliver parcels to customers' doors. It was also his duty to place the parcels in a special section of the tram.

A music hall rhyme of the time went:

She could not find her tramcar fare
The conductor was not rough.
She kissed him sweetly then and there
And he said, 'Fair enough.'

The longest route was from Rathfarnham to Dollymount, and the other extreme was a single-horse route from Ranelagh to Clonskeagh. At certain places with steep gradients, extra 'tip' horses were used to assist the tram. For many years, a big bay horse called Tullamore was kept at Portobello Bridge to help pull the tram over the canal.

Looking south over Portobello bridge, with the Dublin hills in the distance.

The number 15 tram, near its terminus at Nelson's Pillar.

Alas, all things come to an end. Dublin's last horse-drawn tram was operated on 13 January 1901, on the Sandymount line. When the horses were withdrawn, people were afraid they would be electrocuted by the new electric trams. The DUTC pioneered the sending of a high-voltage current from a central power station to local sub-stations, where the voltage was reduced to power the trams. Of course, heavier tramlines had to be laid to accommodate the new tram stock, and this work began in 1896.

Clifton Robinson was a prime mover in the introduction of electric trams. He operated the only independent tram company at the time, called Southern Districts Tramways, which ran from Haddington Road to Dalkey. It was known as the 'English Company', because the said Mr Robinson was from across the Irish Sea. He got the first electric tram going, and then threatened to bring his electric tram inside the canals. Robinson promoted a bill in Parliament to empower him to do so, but this bill met with delays. William Martin Murphy bought out Robinson's company, giving the DUTC a monopoly for the whole city and suburbs.

Dublin Corporation was not initially convinced that electrification of trams was safe. Their qualms were overcome by the DUTC agreeing to maintain the track and eighteen inches on either side of it, and to pay the corporation £500 a year per route mile.

The number 14
tram terminated at
Tramway House.

Terenure Road, Terenure

Terenure Road East,
looking towards
Rathgar village, with
the spire of Christ
Church in the
distance.

The Cars on the Several Routes are distinguished, in addition to the Name Boards on each side and the Destination Indicators at either end, by the Following Signs above the destination Indicators:—

NELSON'S PILLAR AND TERENURE (VIA RATHMINES)	▲	RATHFARNHAM AND DRUMCONDRA (VIA HAROLD'S CROSS)	✖
NELSON'S PILLAR AND DARTRY ROAD (VIA UPPER RATHMINES)	◮	RIALTO AND GLASNEVIN (VIA DOLPHIN'S BARN)	◆
DONNYBROOK AND PHŒNIX PARK (VIA MERRION SQUARE)	◆	NELSON'S PILLAR AND DALKEY	♣
DONNYBROOK AND PHŒNIX PARK (VIA STEPHEN'S GREEN)	◆	NELSON'S PILLAR AND CLONSKEA (VIA LEESON STREET)	◑
KINGSBRIDGE AND HATCH STREET (VIA SOUTHERN QUAYS & WESTLAND ROW)	☐	NELSON'S PILLAR & SANDYMOUNT (VIA RINGSEND)	◡
PARK GATE AND BALLYBOUGH	◆	NELSON'S PILLAR & DOLLYMOUNT	▽
INCHICORE AND WESTLAND ROW	⬬	COLLEGE GREEN & WHITEHALL (VIA CAPEL ST. & DRUMCONDRA)	♡
O'CONNELL BRIDGE & PARK GATE (VIA NORTHERN QUAYS)	☐	KENILWORTH ROAD AND LANSDOWNE ROAD	☐
NELSON'S PILLAR & PALMERSTON PARK	◯		

Each tram line had
its own unique
coloured symbol.

Tramway House, originally the terminus of the number 14 tram, on Dartry Road.

On 19 March 1898, the first electric tram car took passengers from 'the Pillar', i.e. Nelsons Pillar in O'Connell Street, to Dollymount. Within a few short years, the horse-drawn trams were all gone.

The numbering system for trams was introduced in 1918. Number 14 was for Dartry, 15 for Terenure and 16 for Rathfarnham Village. When modern buses were introduced, these numbers were transferred to them. The Terenure tram was number 191. It was known as 'the coffin', because of its hexagonal ends – it was the first tram in the world to have a vestibule front and rear to protect the driver and conductor from the weather.

On the front of each tram was a sign, painted a distinct colour for each route. In the 1911 timetable, a page explains all of the tram signs and colours. The ones we are concerned with are:

Terenure: A red triangle

Dartry Road: A red triangle with a vertical stripe

Palmerston Park: A white circle

Rathfarnham: A green Maltese cross

Stopping places were generally at the first pole beyond each major junction. Each line had its own printed ticket, showing the stages by name. Prescott's Dry Cleaners advertised on the back of all the tickets.

Tram Drivers were a legend in Dublin. They had a reputation for professionalism, and for being polite and cheerful to everyone they came in contact with. They were the captains of the 'tram-ships'. It was a difficult job, as dealing with the public is never easy. They were responsible for everything on and around their tram, and, of course, they had to stand all day.

The trams were big and dominated the road, but the drivers had to contend with the constant danger of colliding with horses or motor cars, both of which would often try to outrun the tram to beat it to a junction. There were accidents constantly, particularly collisions with horses and carts.

The tram driver's worst nightmare was frost, as well as wet leaves on the track in autumn, which could cause the tram to slide when the brakes were applied.

The headlamps on the tram gave very little light, and there were no wipers for the rain. Children 'scutting' (jumping onto the trams) was also a problem, and indeed, some children fell off and were crushed under the trams.

Everything was taken on the tram – prams, bikes, newspaper deliveries, laundry and parcels of all sorts. The conductor rang the bell a specific amount of times to send a message to the driver: one ring meant stop; two rings meant go; three rings meant the tram was full; and four rings signalled an emergency. These same ring combinations continued onto the buses when they took over from the trams.

The electric trams ran successfully until the 1920s, and then fresh competition appeared, in the form of buses. Small bus companies sprang up around the city, and in fact the DUTC obtained a license to operate buses in 1925. In 1939, the regrettable decision was made by the company to run only buses. The last tram to Terenure via Rathgar ran on Halloween 1948. The rails, however, remained on the roads until the late 1960s.

Of course, we now have a light-rail system again in some parts of the city. Now, as then, being located close to a tramline greatly adds to the value of a property.

CHURCHES

As the Rathmines Township expanded to include Rathgar in 1862, it was felt that people needed churches. From 1859 to 1870, a lot of communities were building places of worship. The first was the Religious Society of Friends (Quakers), who built their meeting house across the River Dodder, on Lower Churchtown Road.

Then the Presbyterians built Christ Church at the junction of Rathgar and Highfield roads. This was quickly followed by the Catholic Church of the Three Patrons on Rathgar Road, and the Proprietary Church of Ireland church on Zion Road.

Christ Church Presbyterian church, built in 1860, is the dominant feature in Rathgar village. The men of the Presbyterian community of that time were among the leading businessmen in Dublin: Hugh Moore, a wholesale druggist of 57 Capel Street, lived in Cremorne; Thomas Drury lived in Dartry House; and Robert Bell, of Scott Bell & Company, lived in various houses in Rathgar.

An aerial view of Christ Church, Rathgar, with Rathgar Road on the left and Highfield Road on the right.

ESTABLISHED OVER A CENTURY

W. DRUMMOND & SONS LTD.

Telegrams:
Drummonds Dublin   SEEDSMEN ~ NURSERYMEN AND BULB MERCHANTS

Telephones:
Dublin 45178-45179
(Two Lines)

57 & 58 Dawson Street, DUBLIN

Rev. F. Doherty,

Springfield,   17. 4. *19*42.

Knock, Roscrea, Co. Tipperary.

3 lbs. Mangel, Yellow Globe	12	0
1 bag		6
	12 · 6	
discount		6
	12/-	

CONDITIONS OF SALE.
Although we take every possible care and pains to keep the several varieties of Seeds, Seed Grain and Potatoes we supply pure and true, still we wish it to be distinctly understood that we give no warranty expressed or implied as to their description, quality, productiveness, or any other matter connected with them beyond the declaration required in accordance with the latest "Seed Testing Order," nor will we in any way be responsible for the crop. It must, therefore, be clearly understood that if the purchaser does not accept the goods enumerated here on these terms, they must at once be returned.
W. DRUMMOND & SONS LTD.,
57-58 Dawson Street, Dublin, C 2.

Sold Subject to our conditions of sale as per our current catalogues.

DRUMMOND'S SEEDS

● VAN DELIVERIES ●
CITY AND SUBURBS.

TELEPHONE: DUBLIN 45178/9
57 & 58 DAWSON STREET,
DUBLIN AND CARLOW.

David Drummond lived in Dunfillan
on Orwell Road.

Many house names in Rathgar reflect a Presbyterian ethos, with Scottish names such as Dunfillan, Glengyle and Aberfoyle being prominent. In the 1850s, the Presbyterian congregation met in 89 Upper Rathmines Road. The Church bought the lease from J.J. Lynch on 29 October, 1860.

David Drummond of Drummond Seeds, whose shop was in Dawson Street, lived in Dunfillan, Rathgar, now the St John of God's Lucena Clinic. David was a major driving force in the Presbyterian community in Dublin. Having seen a church that the Hay brothers had built in Sterling in Scotland, David invited the Hays to build the Presbyterian church on Sandymount Green. It was reported at the time that David Drummond had 'imported Hay', and the church in Sandymount became known as 'the Haystack'.

Through his connections with Heiton's coal importers here in Dublin, David Drummond then decided to approach Scottish architect Andrew Heiton (1823–94) to design Christ Church, Rathgar. Heiton also designed the Presbyterian church at York Road in Dún Laoghaire, and the Abbey Church (Findlater's, Rutland Square, now Parnell Square). If you look closely at the York Road church, you will see it is very similar to Christ Church. These churches are copied from St John the Baptist church in Perth, Scotland. Heiton also designed the Mission church in Jervis Street (1864). Heiton, based in Perth, had a huge practice in Scotland and England, his works extending south as far as Leeds.

Above: On the occasion of the opening of Christ Church, Rathgar, 2 February 1862. From left to right: The Reverend Norman MacLeod, D.D., of the Barony Church, Glasgow, Mr J. Cockburn of Messrs. Gilbert Cockburn & Sons (builders) and the Reverend William Fleming Stevenson, D.D.

Above right: Orwell Bank, the original manse for the church.

Right: Rathgar Presbyterian Church Statement of Expenditure.

Christ Church, Rathgar, is in the English Gothic style, and is built of granite and Portland stone. The builder was Gilbert Cockburn, who also built the National Gallery of Ireland and the Natural History Museum in Dublin. Cockburn, an astute man, built the proprietary church in Zion Road at the same time as Christ Church.

The church was opened on 2 February 1862. The first minister was Reverend William Fleming Stevenson (1832–86), from Strabane, County Tyrone. When he came to Rathgar in 1860, he had only about twenty families in his congregation; the figure had increased to 190 before he died. Reverend Stevenson resided first in Leinster Road, and then he rented Orwell Bank, a house belonging to another member of the Presbyterian community, Henry Todd. This was located off what is now Orwell Park. The church bought this house as a Manse, an ecclesiastical residence, in 1878, and owned it until 1898. Orwell Bank, which was demolished in the 1980s, had a fine view of the River Dodder, as described vividly by Reverend Stevenson in his memoirs:

The Dodder a quiet sluggish stream in fair weather, but often rising in a few hours into a foaming mountain torrent which burst its bounds and flooded the fields and rushed down the big weir close to the house with a noise of thunder.

The Dodder flowing sedately by – though it sometimes makes a 'noise of thunder'.

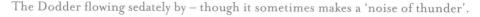

RIVER DODDER RATHGAR DUBLIN

Reverend Stevenson was known internationally as convenor of the church's foreign mission committee. He and his wife travelled 47,000 miles, visiting various missions in Japan, China and India. There is a memorial window in Christ Church, Rathgar, to him. This was made by Cottier and Company in London, and installed in 1888. In 1916, a memorial window to Reverend John Stewart (1862–1913), who succeeded Reverend Stevenson, was installed, designed by Wilhelmina Geddes at An Túr Gloine. Also in the church is a Pulpit Fall designed by Myra Maguire and embroidered by Evelyn Lyndsay, and a memorial to congregants who died in the Great War.

Above: Reverend James Jordan Macauley, fourth minister of Christ Church Rathgar, from 1913 to 1938.
Below: Rathgar Road seen from the under the grand old trees in the grounds of Christ Church.
The shops across the road include antiques, hairstyling, a café, a butcher's, fashion and fine food.

Bushy Park Road, showing Zion Church and School.

In 1867, a major cause of dissension in the Presbyterian congregation was the subject of church music. Some people felt that music devalued the service; others felt it enhanced it. Strong and heated debate continued until in the mid-1880s, when it was resolved to include music in the service.

In 1922, after Saorstát Éireann was formed, Christ Church lost a lot of its Presbyterian community, as several members relocated to Belfast or London. It still has a strong and loyal community.

Zion Church gets its name not from the Church of Ireland, but from the Welsh non-conformist tradition. Zion is the name of one of the seven hills of Jerusalem.

In the 1850s and 1860s, the property owners of Rathgar were unionists, generally Protestant or Dissenter, and very God-fearing. Their attitude was that God was a Protestant and that it was their evangelical duty to convert the godless papists. One of the chief evangelists of the time was Reverend B.W. Matthews. Under his inspiration and influence, the churches of Harold's Cross, Sandford Road, Adelaide Road, Zion Road and Leeson Street were built. These were proprietary churches, i.e. not under the restrictions of the Church of Ireland; they were chapels of ease, and had various conditions put upon them. One of these was that the clergy had to be paid by the trustees of the church, not out of the central funds of the Church of Ireland.

Zion Church was opened on 1 November 1861. According to the census of that year, the population of Rathgar was 1,180. Before the church opened, there was a long dispute, as the trustees had miscalculated the distance between it and Rathfarnham Parish church. One of the conditions of a proprietary church was that it had to be a mile from the nearest parish church, but it was discovered that Zion church was, in fact, only seven furlongs from Rathfarnham Parish church. There was a lot of correspondence in the *Irish Times* about the matter, including an editorial. The opening was delayed by about a year until it was all resolved.

The church was built with a donation from stockbroker John Gold, who lived in Cullenswood in Ranelagh. He was believed to be a member of the Plymouth Brethren. As he had no near relatives, he left money in his will for 'charitable uses'. The trustees of his estate wanted a school with a church and it was said this was why they rejected Christ Church on Rathgar Road. There was no room for a school on that site. A memorial tablets reads:

In memory or John Gold Esq. of Cullenswood Co. Dublin, the founder of this Church and the adjoining schools, who died 28th April, 1855 aged 73 years. His desire in the disposal of his property was to provide a place in which the worship of God should be conducted in simplicity and the Gospel of Our Lord Jesus Christ faithfully preached.

He is buried in Mount Jerome cemetery, Harold's Cross. The inscription on his tomb reads: '... desiring to perpetuate after death his gratitude to God, who had been his guide through life, bequeathed a large portion of his wealth for the erection of Zion Church, Rathgar.'

The seller of the land on the Osbrey estate stated that he would build the roads, Zion church and 350 feet of what is now Bushy Park Road within one year of the sale.

The church was designed by Joseph Welland (1798–1860). He designed more than 100 churches throughout the country, and worked for the Ecclesiastical Commissioners from 1843. It was built at the same time as Christ Church, and by the same builders, Messrs. Cockburn

Zion Church and School, on the corner of Zion Road and Bushy Park Road.

and Son. The cost of building the church and school was £9,600. The trustees of the church received rent of £112 in 1861 from Cullenswood property, which had been owned by Mr Gold. They would also have received income from the rent of the pews. The more prominently your pew was positioned in the church, the higher the rent payable. This was common practice at the time, and ceased in Zion church in 1937.

The Church of Ireland was disestablished on 1 January 1871. In that same year, there was a request that Zion church be changed from a proprietary church to form Rathgar Parish. This wasn't simple, because titles and revenue were tied up, particularly affecting Rathfarnham Parish, who had received considerable revenue from the Rathgar area. Parish income would be affected. The situation was finally resolved after fourteen years of division and dispute, and Rathgar Parish was formed in 1885.

The first minister of Zion church was Reverend James Hewitt, a graduate of Trinity College, Dublin. He served as a curate in England and, after returning to Ireland, was assistant minister

An arched entrance to Rathfarnham Castle, now sadly gone.

in Harold's Cross (1854–57) and St Matthias's Church, Adelaide Road (1858–61), until his appointment to Zion church, aged thirty-three. He served the church until his death in 1895, aged sixty-seven. There is a brass lectern is his honour, reading 'In memory of our beloved Pastor, the Rev. James Hewitt, M.A.'

There is a Roll of Honour to the eighty-six members of the congregation who 'jeopardised their lives unto death' in the Great War. In fact, seventeen members were killed.

In 1966, Zion school was the largest Church of Ireland school in the Republic, with 246 pupils on the roll.

In 1859, a meeting was called by Dr Osbbrey (sic) to decide where a new bridge should cross the Dodder. Most people wanted the existing Waldron's wooden bridge to be replaced, but there were strong objections from Mr Blackburn of Rathfarnham Demesne. He felt the road should go through his estate, and he wanted the bridge to cross the Dodder at Ely Gate, where the pedestrian bridge is now. The road would go straight down Zion Road, through what is now the High School, to the Dodder. He obviously wanted compensation.

It was decided that the bridge would go where it is now (Orwell Bridge), but that residents would have to lay out the road themselves. However, a Mr Waldron, who lived at the Dodder on Orwell Road, got the residents to resurface the road and build a wooden bridge to cross the river. It seems perhaps that the trustees of Zion church miscalculated, thinking Zion Road would be the main road.

Left: River Dodder at Orwell Gardens, and the bridge to Smokey Hollow. Flooding was a serious problem here for many years.
Below: Orwell Bridge, which replaced the wooden Waldron's Bridge.

The Baptist Church
on Grosvenor Road.

M O'BRIEN 2019©

GROSVENOR ROAD BAPTIST CHURCH

The Baptist church on Grosvenor Road was designed by Carmichael and Jones, and built in 1859. Once again, this is an example of a church being built to serve hoped-for prospective buyers in the area.

The Baptist movement came to Ireland in the 1650s. There are now over 100 Baptist churches in Ireland. The Irish Baptist Church is an autonomous church, having broken away from Britain in 1895. Baptists are not a denomination, as each church is a separate entity, but they share a common bond. They are an evangelical church, whose members are baptised as adults.

RATHGAR METHODIST CHURCH, BRIGHTON ROAD

The first Methodist church in south Dublin was built at the corner of Charleston Road in Ranelagh in 1801. Some years later, a larger church was built near Belgrave Square. As the suburbs extended further, it was felt that another church was needed. In 1874, the Brighton Road site was obtained, and a small church was built on the site, described in the papers as 'the new Wesleyan church'.

The foundation stone was laid on 12 February 1874. Interestingly, under the foundation stone, a wide glass bottle was laid, containing all the newspapers of the day and the names of the building committee.

In 1885, there were thirty buildings on Brighton Square, and in 1900 this had expanded to seventy-one, illustrating how the area was developing.

The Methodist Church cost £2,239 to build, and seated 285 people. It was opened on Friday, 7 August 1874. Then in 1879, the Manse Lecture Hall and the sexton's apartments were built by the Beckett brothers, one of whom, William, was the father of author and playwright Samuel Beckett.

There were further additions in 1892, including the spire being added. In 1910, the church was extended to include a war memorial window and, in 1914, a bigger lecture hall was built. The architect was R. Caulfield Orpen. The war memorial window was constructed by Messrs Heaton Butler & Boyne of London, and it cost £619. In the 1960s, a fête was held in the church to raise money for overseas missions, a tradition still carried on today.

The Church of the Three Patrons on Rathgar Road,
formerly known as the Servants' Church. The three patrons
are of course saints Patrick, Brigid and Columba.

THE THREE PATRONS CHURCH

With the development of the Rathgar area during the 1860s came the need for a place of worship for Roman Catholics. Although there were Catholics in the area who owned houses, the vast majority were servants, who amounted to about a quarter of the population. In the 1871, 1881 and 1891 censuses, there were more Catholics than Protestants in the Rathmines and Rathgar Township.

A wealthy Catholic parishioner bequeathed £2,000 to the parish priest of Rathmines to build a church in Rathgar. Catholic parishes evolved in Dublin as the population spread out from the city. Generally, new churches were designated as chapels of ease of the previous parish. Hence, Rathgar's new Three Patrons Church became the chapel of ease of Rathmines. It did not become a parish church till 1882. The three patrons of Ireland are Saint Patrick, Saint Bridget and Saint Columba/Columcille.

The parish priest of Rathmines from 1848 to 1881 was Father William Meagher. Having modernised Rathmines church, he changed its name in 1856 from Saints Mary and Peter to Mary Immaculate Refuge of Sinners. (The declaration of 'immaculate conception' was made dogma in 1854). Father Meagher was aware that some servants were not being given enough time to attend Mass on Sundays in Rathmines, so he set about building the church in Rathgar.

The Church of the Three Patrons.

He obtained a corner plot for £550. He obtained £4,650 from various sources, including a personal loan of £1,500 from Archbishop Paul Cullen that Father Meagher repaid out of his own income. When the foundation stone was laid, on 17 March 1860, the *Irish Times* reported that there were scenes of 'mob fanaticism and priestly display'. 'A chapel, it seems, is to depreciate the value of the property of the neighbourhood and to drive the Protestant occupants from the place.' Despite protests from neighbours, the building went ahead.

As can be plainly seen, it is a fairly restricted site. The front elevation, in the neo-classical style, wasn't erected until the 1890s. The inscription in Latin reads, 'D.O.M. Sub Invoca. Trium. Hiberniae. S. S. Protector', which translates as, 'To God the best and the greatest under the invocation of the three patron saints of Ireland'.

Above and left: Originally called Oaklands, the home of printer and stationer Charles Wisdom Hely on Highfield Road, this beautiful house, with its ornate plasterwork and immaculately kept grounds is now St Luke's Hospital.

The Church was designed by architect Patrick Byrne, in the style of a Roman basilica. Byrne had designed other churches in Dublin, including Rathmines Parish church, the Church of Mary Immaculate, Refuge of Sinners. It is felt that his original plans for the Three Patrons Church were altered, whether by Father Meagher or somebody else. Inside, it is a beautiful, welcoming church, worthy of a visit.

HIGHFIELD ROAD

Highfield Road was originally referred to as the 'Old Rathgar Road', and then Cross Avenue, before finally becoming Highfield Road. The main house in the area was Rathgar House, situated on the St Luke's Hospital site.

RATHGAR HOUSE, OAKLANDS, ST LUKE'S HOSPITAL

The original house was built by Richard Wilson. He sold it to Charles Farren, who was Clerk of the Pleas of Court of the Exchequer. When Farren died in 1808, he was succeeded by his son Joseph. Reggie Redmond, in his pamphlet 'The History of Oakland Rathgar', states that Joseph is most likely to have constructed the house we have now.

Joseph's two sisters Barbara and Louisa, who lived with him, designed a beautiful little house decorated with sea shells they had collected in Balbriggan between 1834 and 1861. Conchology, as the collection of shells is known, was a fashionable pastime at the time. The majority of the shells collected in Ireland were bivalves, i.e. having two shell halves, like mussels or scallops. The remains of another shell house can still be seen in the woods of Bushy Park.

The shell house stood in the grounds of Oaklands until about 1950, when a workman misunderstood instructions and demolished part of it. The little house then fell into disrepair, and is now gone. When Rathgar House was sold in 1853, the sisters moved to Georgeville, 16 Highfield Road, but they continued to have access to their shell house until they died.

Henry Todd, of Todd, Burns & Co.'s famous drapery shop in Mary Street, bought Rathgar House, and renamed it Oakland. Another Rathgar House was located on Bushy Park Road, and yet another where Orwell nursing home is now. Later on, another Rathgar House was built at the bottom of Rathgar Avenue.

Mr Todd didn't last long in the house, and it was sold around 1864 to Hugh Brown, who had been a buyer with Mr Todd. Another buyer in Todd's was James Thomas. Brown and Thomas went into partnership and formed a shop, Brown Thomas & Co. This is the iconic store in Grafton Street, now located across the road from its original site, where Marks & Spencer is now.

When Brown, died his widow Marianne moved to Glengyle on Orwell Road, and lived there until 1892. This is now Stratford College. Their son, Robert, was a doctor and established his practice at Hopeton, 33 Terenure Road East. A window is dedicated to him in Zion church; he added an 'e' to his name, becoming Browne.

Oakland was bought in 1893 by Charles Wisdom Hely, who was Managing Director of Hely Printers and Stationers, 28 Dame Street. His firm was one of the biggest printers and stationers in Dublin. His monogram is still on the rear gates of Saint Luke's hospital, leading to Orwell Park. In 1901, Hely had one of the first cars in Ireland, a Panhard, which had people terrified with its top speed of 30mph. He was Vice-President of the Royal Irish Automobile Club, and was also a major shareholder in the Dunlop company.

He improved the gardens of Oakland, and built a heated greenhouse. The gardens included a croquet lawn and a tennis court. Hely employed four gardeners to tend the grounds and keep the house supplied with fresh vegetables. Gardening was an important part of the social fabric of society then. Royal Horticultural Society medals and cups were highly prized, at both local and national level. Hely often won prizes.

Charles Hely died in 1929, and his wife Edith May sold part of the driveway to James Steward, a builder, who lived in Fortfield House in Rathmines. The gates were moved back from Highfield Road to where they are now.

Their daughter Violet married Major Johnnie O'Rourke, and they sold the estate to the Irish Cancer Association of Ireland in 1950, for £26,000. In 1901, Violet was a teenage motorist until the 1904 Act denied her a licence, being underage.

At the crossroads in Rathgar we now have shops, restaurants and pubs. In the late 1700s, there was a pub here called The Thatch. Travellers coming to Dublin, particularly from the southeast, used to refer to Rathgar as 'The Thatch'. This was the first stop for many on reaching Dublin. Before the advent of trains, horse-drawn carriages were the only form of transport. These were slow and uncomfortable. You paid a cheaper fare if you travelled outside, exposed to the vagaries of the Irish weather. So The Thatch was a welcome sight, where you got the original Irish breakfast.

Orwell Road, just south of Rathgar crossroads, showing the The Flower Bowl florists, SuperValu and Runzone running shop.

Above: Orlando, an abandoned house on Orwell Road, has lain empty and derelict for many years. The Dalrymple family lived here years ago. A planning application to build five houses on the site was refused in 2019.

Below: The Lucena Clinic, originally Dunfillan.

ORWELL ROAD

DUNFILLAN, ORWELL ROAD, NOW THE LUCENA CLINIC

David Drummond's family had an 'agricultural museum' in Stirling, Scotland, which specialised in seeds. David came to Ireland in 1834, setting up business at 57 Dawson Street. The business grew to become one of the most successful in the city. Like many businessmen before and since, he decided in invest in other projects. He was a director of the Alliance & Dublin Consumers' Gas Company, Dublin United Tramways Company and the Royal Bank of Ireland. He was on the board of the Royal Hospital, Donnybrook, the Lying-in Hospital in the Coombe, the Royal Victoria Eye and Ear Hospital and St Andrew's College. He was a member of the Winter Garden Company, formed to set up the Great Industrial Exhibition of 1853, with William Dargan as its Chairman. Drummond was a member of the Dublin Chamber of Commerce, a Justice of the Peace and a very active member of the temperance movement.

When he died in 1904, he left an estate of £49,000 to divide among his five children. He spared no effort in building Dunfillan, including building a 'gentleman's crystal palace', i.e. a greenhouse, thought to have been designed and built by Richard Turner or an associate of his.

Due to his background, Drummond was a judge at many horticultural shows, including at the RDS and the Royal Horticultural Society of Ireland. He mainly judged fruit and vegetables.

Dunfillan was eventually sold to a publican, Mr Murphy. He owned the pub which is now the '108' in Rathgar. His widow sold Dunfillan

The quarry and windmill at Windmill Road, now Orwell Road, in a dramatic painting by George Petrie.

to the St John of God brothers in the early 1950s. It was renamed Lucena, and is now a St John of God family clinic. It takes its name from the first hospital set up by St John of God, in 1539 in Granada, Spain. In 1952/53 the Department of Health approached the St John of God brothers, asking them to set up a child guidance clinic. The first child attended it on 5 September 1955.

* * *

Rathgar Avenue came from Harold's Cross to Rathgar, and then on to the Dodder via a small pathway where Orwell Road is now.

The Rathgar Tennis Club in Herzog Park, Orwell Road, is located where there had been an extensive limestone quarry. There was a huge pump to keep the quarry free of water, and this was powered by a large windmill. The road was originally called Windmill Road.

This brings up another contentious issue. As I stated, the Presbyterian community included some of the most influential men in Dublin. In 1862, some of these were on the Board of what had now become the Rathmines and Rathgar Township. They had seen the members of the Zion church name the road Zion Road. In 1864, the Township decided to change the name of Windmill Road to Orwell Road. Why 'Orwell'? The question has always intrigued me, as all the other roads in the area aped English placenames.

The answer comes from the Presbyterian community. In Perthshire, Scotland, there is a ruin of a church called Orwell Kirk. This drew its name from an estate on the banks of Loch Leven, about two miles northeast of Kinross. The Scots claim the word Orwell comes from a Scots Gaelic term for 'a green or fertile retreat'. The people of the church of Orwell had a history of dissension, having broken away and rejoined the established Church several times; they joined the Free Church of Scotland in 1843, and the United Presbyterian Church in 1847.

David Drummond was from Scotland, and it is likely that he influenced the change of name. Perhaps there was an element of triumphalism here, as Orwell Road was now the main road to Churchtown, rather than Zion Road as had been proposed in the early 1860s.

* * *

These old setts represent a
crossing place, where you
could avoid getting the hem of
your frock dusty.

Orwell Road initially had entrance gates. These were removed in 1886, but the pillars remained in place until 1912.

In 1832, the quarry was owned by Mr Osbrey, and in 1842, John Whitford owned it. In 1863, it became the property of John Bond, who lived in Victoria Villa, where the Rathgar branch of the Allied Irish Bank is now. The limestone was not of great quality, too poor to be used as finished stone. It was used for building walls that would be plastered, or for garden walls, and examples of this local limestone can be seen in garden walls all over Rathgar. Sometimes referred to as 'black stone', it was often the curse of builders, as it is difficult to drill through.

Limestone from the quarry was also used for road surfacing, being ground down to 'calp' and spread on the roads. The roads could thus be extremely dusty in summer, and very mucky in winter. Ladies had to hold up their dresses, and setts were put in the roads at crossings. Of course, a lot of houses had foot scrapers at the hall door, to be used before entering the house.

One Mr Jordan, a road contractor, lived in Airfield, off Rathgar Avenue. In the 1890s, the quarry was known as Jordan's Quarry. The Rathgar Stone Company, as it was called, ceased trading in 1906. The quarry then filled up with water. Dublin Corporation eventually filled it in, firstly with only dry filling but in the 1950s in order to speed up the filling all refuse was allowed, bringing with it lots of rats. Then the locals referred to Ratgar! In 1962, while dumping a load, James Kinsella backed his lorry into the quarry and was unfortunately drowned. Finally, when it was filled after much persuasion, the Corporation turned the quarry into a park, called Herzog Park.

Washerwoman's Lane from the Orwell Road end.

Herzog Park was named after Chaim Herzog. His father, Yitzhak, was Chief Rabbi of Ireland from 1919 to 1937. He was known as 'the Sinn Féin rabbi', and was a fluent Irish speaker. His son Chaim was born in Belfast, but grew up in Bloomfield Avenue, South Circular Road. Chaim went to school in Wesley College, which was then in St Stephen's Green. Chaim emigrated to Palestine in 1935, but later moved to London and qualified as a lawyer. He joined the British Army as a tank commander in the Second World War. There he got the nickname 'Vivian', as the English could not pronounce Chaim.

He returned to Palestine after the war, and fought to establish the State of Israel. Chaim then opened a law practice, and subsequently established the law firm of Herzog, Fox & Neeman, still one of the biggest law firms in Israel today. In 1981, he entered politics and was elected to the Knesset, Israel's parliament. On 22 March 1983, he was elected President of Israel.

Rathgar Tennis Club occupies part of Herzog Park. Founded in 1985, it is a wonderful amenity for the area.

Stratford College on Zion Road, Dublin's Jewish school, was originally a house called Orbiston.

Heading south down Orwell Road from Rathgar village, the first lane on the left is Washerwoman's Lane, which got its name from the occupation of the women who lived there. The lane goes all the way to St Luke's Hospital, running at the back of the houses. There was a row of cottages on the land, called Orwell Cottages.

At the junction of Orwell Road and Zion Road, this house was originally called Rostrevor.

ZION ROAD

Stratford College was originally called Orbiston, named after another place in Scotland. Orbiston was the home of the Owenite Community (1825–28), set up by the social reformer Robert Owen. Thomas Wardrop, another stalwart of Christ Church, lived here. He was a contractor, at Wardrop and Sons, Conyngham Road. His works included the building of the reservoir in Gallanstown on the canal, to supply water to the Township. He also built the retaining wall on the river Liffey between Victoria Bridge and Kingsbridge, and many other large contracts.

This house was refurbished by Marianne Brown when she moved from Oakland in 1892, and she changed its name to Glengyle.

In the 1950s, the Jewish community of Dublin decided to start a secondary school for their children. It was located at 59 Terenure Road East, in a house called Stratford. When the opportunity presented itself, Glengyle was bought and the school moved here in 1954. Stratford College was nearly burned down in a fire in 1979, but it opened its new building in 1981. Over the years, Dublin's Jewish community has decreased. Although Stratford College still retains its Jewish ethos, it accepts pupils of all faiths.

Above: A ration ticket, dating from famine times. Left: A terrace of Victorian houses on Victoria Road. Number 20 is the home of the publisher.

VICTORIA ROAD

This road was built on the Cremorne Estate, with the builders paying homage to England's Queen Victoria, who died in January 1901. The first houses were sold in October of the same year. The 1901 census shows that there are three houses on the road, two occupied by Smith Builders.

The influence of street preaching was evident in the 1840s, and of course trying to convert papists was a major priority. At this time, during the Irish 'famine', the expression to 'take the soup' meant converting religion in order to be fed. A place where soup was given out by evangelists was referred to by Catholics as a 'crow's nest'.

Jimmy O'Dea, comedian of the Dublin stage in the 1940s, 1950s and 1960s, used to say, 'Rathgar is a purgatory for souls awaiting the heaven of Foxrock.'

Number 4 Zion Road, home of the le Brocquy
family, who ran the Greenmount Oil Company.

BACK ON ZION ROAD

Number 4 Zion Road is where Louis le Brocquy (1916–2012) was born. The opening lines of his biography *Seeing His Way*, written by his wife Anne Madden, state, 'Louis was born to Sybil, née de Lacy Staunton, and Albert le Brocquy at 6am on Friday 10 November 1916 at 4 Zion Road, Rathgar, Dublin, in the middle of World War I during the year of the Easter Rising.'

The book goes on to tell of his maternal uncle Herbert, who died from a kick in the head received while playing rugby. Le Brocquy's grandfather had been injured in a fire, and he came to Zion Road to recover. Again, it was his head that had been injured. Could these embedded childhood memories have been a source for his numerous later paintings of heads? Le Brocquy said that seeing primitive heads in a museum in Paris had inspired him to paint heads in this style.

He was born into a wealthy family. In 1887, his grandfather, also Louis, set up an oil refinery in Ringsend. When this burned down in 1896, he founded the Greenmount Oil Company in Harold's Cross. Louis's father later became secretary of the company. Le Brocquy attended Mount Temple kindergarten, Palmerstown Road, where his art teacher was Elizabeth (Lolly) Yeats. From there he went to St Gerard's School in Bray. The family moved to 51 Kenilworth Square, although le Brocquy finished his education in St Gerard's in Bray. He then started working in the oil company, while studying Chemistry in Trinity College.

His main interest, however, always lay in painting. Largely self-taught, he mainly learned his craft on the continent. In 1938, he went to Paris with his then-girlfriend Jean Stoney, marrying in London on the way. They eventually settled in the south of France, and le Brocquy began to paint and to consider himself a painter.

Their daughter Seyre was born on 4 June 1939. The Second World War broke out that September, and the couple returned to Dublin. Their marriage lasted just two and a half years.

Helped by his family connections, le Brocquy had begun to paint portraits. In 1941, he painted 'Girl in White', a portrait of film star Kathleen Ryan, whose family lived on Orwell Road. The painting is now in the Ulster Museum in Belfast.

Louis and his sister Melanie, who was a sculptor, had adjoining studios at Merrion Row, and held their first joint exhibition in 1942. The following year, feeling that there was no proper place to exhibit art in Ireland, le Brocquy, with fellow artists Mainie Jellett, Evie Hone, Norah McGuinness, Ralph Cusack and Reverend Jack Hanlon, set up the Irish Exhibition of Living Art.

Le Brocquy continued to paint, mainly in the south of France. He also illustrated books, notably Thomas Kinsella's *The Táin* and James Joyce's *Dubliners*. In the 1960s, he met and married Anne Madden and they had two children, Pierre and Alexis. Le Brocquy was the first living Irish artist whose work was sold for over €1 million. His final home and studio was in Longwood Avenue, South Circular Road.

Lisnamae, number 24 Zion Road, was the home of Robert Lloyd Praeger (1865–1953). Robert was born in Hollywood, County Down. His father was a Dutch linen merchant, but his interest in nature originated from his mother's side. She was Marie Patterson, daughter of the naturalist Robert Patterson (1802–72). One of a family of four boys and one girl, Robert qualified as an engineer and got his first job with the Belfast Waterworks in 1886. He found the job boring though, just as he had found school boring.

Praeger eked out a living on contracts, but at the same time published the first of over 800 papers. The National Library of Ireland, which opened in 1890, gave him a job as assistant librarian. He became the chief librarian in 1920, before availing of the Treaty amnesty for civil servants and retiring in 1923. All the time he had been writing papers and books on natural Ireland. He had co-founded the *Irish Naturalist* journal with George Carpenter in 1905.

In 1901, while on holiday in Germany, he met Hedwig Elena Ingeborg Meta Magnusson, an artist's daughter. At the end of his two-week holiday, they became engaged, marrying the following year and moving into 24 Zion Road. She was a constant companion and great support to him all his life. They had no children.

Praeger completed his first survey of the flora and fauna of Lambay Island in 1905–06. He then went on to do his definitive Clare Island Survey in 1909–11, a highly detailed study undertaken under the auspices of the Royal Irish Academy. It covered archaeology, agriculture, botany, climatology, geology and zoology. This survey has been repeated by the RIA within the last few years.

The 1880 entrance gates to Danum on Zion Road, the Bewleys' farm, famous for its Jersey cattle. The High School moved here in 1971, and the Diocesan School for Girls merged with them in 1974.

His book *The Way That I Went* was published in 1937, and to this day remains one of the best guide books on Ireland. In 1941, he published his autobiography, *A Populous Solitude*. He describes his quarter-acre garden at 24 Zion Road:

> One half of that area was occupied by the house itself, paths and grass. The remainder was free, and by degrees most of it was converted into rock-garden, the rest being occupied by herbaceous plants and flowering shrubs ... The list of names, mostly of distinct species, in my garden book ran to some two thousand ...

He adds that he gave 2,000 of the less hardy shrubs to the Botanic Gardens at Glasnevin.

When he left Zion Road, he went to live in 27 Fitzwilliam Square. Following his wife's death in 1952, he went back to Craigavad, County Down, to live with his sister Rosamund. He worked right up to his death, and his last book, *The Irish Landscape*, was published in 1953. Praeger is buried with his wife in Deansgrange Cemetery, although in his book, *The Way That I Went*, he expresses a wish to be buried in County Down.

The Bewley family.

His sister Sophia Rosamund (1867–1954) was a renowned painter and illustrator. She and her brother were very close, and she illustrated his works *Open Air Studies in Botany* (1897) and *Weeds: Simple lessons for children* (1913). Another brother, William, became Professor of Biology and Geology in Kalamazoo University, Michigan, in 1905.

The High School, Danum, is located at the end of Zion Road. In the early 1900s, the Bewley family bought a farm here, and they built a house on it called Danum. The name comes from the Latin for Doncaster, where the Bewley family originated. It was here that Ernest Bewley farmed his herd of Jersey cows, providing the milk, cream and butter for the famous Bewley's cafés.

The family were members of the Religious Society of Friends (Quakers). Charles Bewley and his son Joshua started their business, the China Tea Company, in 1840, in Sycamore Alley off Dame Street, before Joshua moved to 13 South Great George's Street. Feeling that he would not be able to earn a living from just tea and coffee, he also imported oriental vases, delph and ornaments from 1894 onwards, the same year that the first Bewleys café opened.

Joshua's son Ernest, who took over the business, would grind and roast the coffee beans at the back of the shop, and the delicious aroma would encourage people to come in and make a purchase. Ernest bought 10 Westmoreland Street in 1896, and in 1900 bought 19/20 Fleet Street, setting up a bicycle shop in partnership with another man. When his partner withdrew, Ernest turned it into a café.

In 1926, the name was changed from Charles Bewley and Company to Bewley's Oriental Cafés Ltd. This same year, they acquired 78/79 Grafton Street, the site of Samuel Whyte's English Grammar School, founded in 1758. It was here that Harry Clarke was commissioned to design his six magnificent stained glass windows.

Danum was a successful farm, and even had its own cricket team. A lot of the big estates had cricket teams, and the rivalry between them was intense. It was not beyond people to bring in 'ringers' – good players who were not estate workers! In the 1950s, Danum was split into Danum Meadows, where A.C. Bewley lived, and Danum Firs, where Victor E. Bewley lived. In 1969, the Bewleys transferred their Jersey herd to a newly acquired farm in Moyvalley, County Kildare, and The High School moved to Danum.

The High School was set up thanks to the munificence of Erasmus Smith, a Cromwellian adventurer, who made his money selling corn to Cromwell's troops. Using his bequest, schools were set up all over the country, but most have since closed.

In 1870, the Board of Governors of the Erasmus Smith Trust set up The High School in Harcourt Street, for 'ordinary people of Dublin'. The new school at Danum was officially opened by An Taoiseach, Jack Lynch, on 26 November 1971. It is intriguing that at just about the same time, the Protestant schools in that area of Dublin – The High School, Wesley College, Alexandra College and the Diocesan School – all moved to the suburbs. The High School became co-educational in 1974 when it amalgamated with the Diocesan Girls' School.

One of the past pupils of The High School was the poet W.B. Yeats. His main interest in school was natural history studies, and he began writing poetry during his last year in school, in 1883.

An old farmhouse in one of the quiet lanes in the area.

69

When he left The High School, he attended the National College of Art in Kildare Street. He went on to win a Nobel Prize for Literature in 1923.

Sixty-nine High School old boys were killed during the Great War, and a stained glass window was installed in Harcourt Terrace to honour the dead. It was designed and made by W. Mac Bride of Craft Workers Ltd., 39 Harcourt Street, who also created the memorial window in St Patrick's Cathedral. The window was transferred to Danum when the school moved.

BUSHY PARK ROAD

This road was originally just a pathway, at the end of which was a gate to Bushy Park Estate. The name comes from the Shaw residence on Templeogue Road, Rathfarnham.

In the early 1840s, Bushy Park Road was composed of a few big estates. On the left were Willow Bank and Meadowbank, the latter owned by a Mr Copperthwaite. Beyond that, in Terenure, were Riversdale and Eastbourne.

Just past Zion Church on Bushy Park Road was Prospect House, on the lands of which another Rathgar House (1867) was built by Mr Simonton. He was a photographer–optician, with the title 'Royal Panopticon of Science and Art', at 70 Grafton Street.

Number 7 was the home of Walter Fox. His father, James J. Fox, ran his cigar merchant's shop at 119 Grafton Street. James had worked for the previous owners of the premises, the Maddens. James Madden blended tobaccos, particularly for pipe smokers. When James Madden died in 1878, the premises closed, and in the following three years, it was rebuilt. In 1881, James Fox obtained the lease to the ground floor of the new premises. Astutely, he opened in early December, which was always the busiest time of the year for business. Fox then extended the business into the flourishing cigar trade.

The smoking public who frequented his shop were of title and rank, and the business continued to grow. In 1914, Walter moved into 7 Bushy Park Road. His father, James, lived with him until James's death in 1916. Walter was forty-six years of age when he inherited the business. Walter married Maud Luke, whose father was headmaster of Dublin's Metropolitan School of Art, which became the National College of Art and Design (NCAD).

At 7.15pm on 1 January 1926, Walter and his eldest son Stanley, returning home from the shop, were stopped by three men at the corner of Zion Road. Armed with revolvers, the men were eyeing a 'Gladstone' bag Stanley was carrying. Stanley grappled with one of the men, catching him around the neck. The thief shot Stanley in the stomach. Walter was hit on the head with a revolver butt. The robbers seized the bag and ran. Stanley was taken to St Patrick Dun's Hospital, where he died four days later. The robbers were never apprehended, and furthermore, the bag had only contained a few papers and cigarettes.

Walter died four years later, and his wife Maud took control of the business. Aware of her limitations, she appointed Kevin Charles Shelley as manager. Her sons Biffy and Fred came into the trade under Shelley, who lived in Grove Park, Rathmines. He was the founder of the Catholic Boy Scouts, and the only Roman Catholic to work in Fox's.

The business continues to the fifth generation today. Still trading at 119 Grafton Street, it has now expanded to provide whiskey and other products.

Number 12 is where Erskine Childers (1870–1922) lived, the father of President Erskine Childers. Erskine senior was born in London, and worked as a clerk in the House of Commons from 1895 to 1910). He later volunteered and served in the Boer War in South Africa. He married an American heiress, Mary Ellen Osgood, and their wedding present from her parents was the yacht *Asgard*. This was the boat that was used to bring arms to Howth for the Irish Volunteers in 1914, and many years later became a training vessel for young people interested in sailing. It is now on display in the National Museum, Collins Barracks.

Erskine's mother's people were Bartons of Glendalough House, County Wicklow. He had spent several holidays there, and regarded this house as his true home. Having run guns to Howth, he then enlisted in the Royal Navy at the outbreak of the First World War. After the war, he returned to the Irish nationalist cause. In the first Dáil (1919), he was elected as a Sinn Féin TD for County Wicklow, and was appointed director of publicity. Being English, he was always suspected of being a spy.

Dodder Bank, Rathgar, Co. Dublin

The verdant banks of the Dodder.

He was one of the secretaries to the plenipotentiaries during the Treaty negotiations, in which his cousin Robert Barton was one of the main delegates. He opposed the Treaty. In 1922, during the Civil War, he was arrested in Glendalough House, and tried in a military court for being in possession of a gun that he had been given by Michael Collins. He was executed in Beggar's Bush Barracks, Dublin. In 1964, his wife donated his papers to the State, requesting that they not be opened for fifty years.

BACK ON ORWELL ROAD

Stratford House, on six acres, was occupied by Sir Edward Hutchinson Synge (1830–1906), 4th Baronet Hutchinson. He fought in the Crimean War, and died at the age of seventy-six, unmarried. The house was occupied in the 1880s by Jonathon Hogg, a merchant with a business at 12 Cope Street.

Aberfoyle (later Carrick Hall), Ashmere and Rockdale on Orwell Road, built by
developer and seed merchant David Drummond for his sons.

An old man called Jack Switzer used to live in the gate lodge here. He was known as 'the father
of the Dodder', and was involved in setting up the Dublin Anglers' Association. He fought in the
First World War, and taught children to fish in the 1930s and 1940s. His stories about the war
used to include, 'And do you know what, lads? When the bomb exploded in the river, the fish used
to leap out of it and I could catch them in my helmet.'

In the 1860s, the lands of Dunfillan extended along Orwell Road where David Drummond's
sons built three houses for his family – Aberfoyle, Rockdale and Ashmere. These houses are now
numbers 69, 71 and 73 Orwell Road.

Number 69, Aberfoyle, was occupied by Sir Howard Grubb (1844–1931) from 1905 to 1925,
after which he moved to De Vesci Terrace, Dún Laoghaire.

Howard's father Thomas Grubb (1800–78), a County Waterford man, opened a business in
Dublin, designing and printing notes for the Bank of Ireland. He also won a silver medal at the

Royal Dublin Society in 1835 for designing a cast-iron billiard table. He worked as an optician, and then made refracting telescopes. Thomas helped to build the famous telescope for William Parsons at Birr Castle, County Offaly, and built a public observatory near his factory at 1 Upper Charlemont Street. He worked mainly from a premises in Ranelagh, and then moved his works to Rathmines in the 1860s, where it occupied a place next door to Leinster Cricket Grounds, called Observatory Lane.

In 1834, with the help of Reverend Thomas Romney Robinson of Armagh Observatory, he constructed a fifteen-inch reflecting telescope, incorporating several innovations:

It was the first to be mounted on a polar axis with a clock drive.

It had a novel lever support system for the primary mirror.

It was a Cassegrain telescope, rather than a Newtonian.

You had to be perched on top of a Newtonian telescope to view the sky, as the eyepiece was mounted to the side, whereas with the Cassegrain, you could stand on the ground. The mirrors were made of an alloy of copper and tin called speculum metal. This was extremely fragile, but excellent for its high reflectivity.

Thomas Grubb lived in Leinster Square and Leinster Road. His son Howard first lived in Kenilworth Square, and then moved to Orwell Road. Howard studied engineering at Trinity College, but with his father's business expanding, left before qualifying, taking over the business completely in 1876.

Howard continued to make telescopes, making the largest in the UK in 1893 for the Royal Observatory, Greenwich. In 1900, he developed 'reflex' or 'reflector sight', which was used in all kinds of weaponry and armaments. He also developed the periscope for submarines.

Howard was Town Commissioner of Rathmines, and Governor of the National Gallery. An active member of the Royal Dublin Society (RDS), his roles included Secretary (1889–93) and President (1893–1922). He received the medal of the Society, the 'Boyle Medal', in 1912, the third member to receive this honour. After the 1916 Rising, feeling concerned and indeed threatened, he moved his business to St Alban's in England. The business did not go well there, and he amalgamated with Sir Charles Parsons of Birr, the Earl of Rosse's third son. He died in 1931, and was buried in Dean's Grange Cemetery.

Aberfoyle was then occupied by John Marcus O'Sullivan (1881–1948). Born in Kerry, he was educated in St Brendan's College in Killarney and Clongowes Wood College, County Kildare. He obtained his degree from the Royal University of Ireland, founded in 1880 and dissolved in 1909. O'Sullivan received a philosophical scholarship to Bonn and Heidelberg universities. In 1910, with the foundation of UCD, he was appointed to the chair of Modern History, a position he held until his death.

In 1923, he was elected a Cumann na nGaedheal TD for North Kerry. He was parliamentary secretary to the Minister of Finance in 1924, and became Minister for Education in 1926. He lost his seat in 1943. O'Sullivan is remembered as the man who introduced the Vocational Education Act of 1930. It set up thirty-eight Vocational Education Committees (VECs). This is commemorated annually in Kerry with the John Marcus O'Sullivan Summer School.

The house was renamed Carrick Hall in the 1960s. Initially it was run as apartments, which were leased on a short-term basis. It was then run as a hotel by Colm and Margret Rice, but with the downturn in the economy it ceased trading. It is now a private residence again.

Number 71, Rockdale, was the home of Edward Dowden (1843–1913), Professor of Oratory and English Literature.

In 1875, Dowden's reputation went around the world with his book *Shakspere: A critical study of his mind and art*, which was translated into German and Russian. He lectured in Oxford between 1890 and 1893, and in Cambridge from 1893 to 1896. He wrote more than thirty books on English literature, and was regarded as one of the foremost international authorities on Shakespeare. It is felt that in Joyce's *Ulysses*, Stephen Dedalus's thoughts in the National Library are Dowden's thoughts. He also wrote *A Life of Shelley*.

Dowden was a fervent anti-nationalist, and was totally against Home Rule. As a professor in Trinity College, he was mentor to Bram Stoker, and both championed the poet Walt Whitman (1819–92).

Number 71, Rockdale, was home to Séamus and Agnes Ryan and their family. The Ryans were well known as the owners of the Monument Creameries, a chain of cafés/shops – the Starbucks of their time. Séamus Ryan and his wife Agnes (née Harding), of County Tipperary, opened their first shop in Parnell Street in 1918, taking the name from the famous Parnell monument at the top of O'Connell Street.

The business expanded to thirty-six outlets. Séamus was a republican, and during the War of Independence, hid IRA Volunteers on the run from British forces in his shop. He was a founder of the Fianna Fáil party in 1926, and a generous donor. Elected a senator in 1931, he died two years later, at the age of thirty-seven. He was given a State funeral, and is buried in the republican plot in Glasnevin. His wife Agnes was a great patron of the arts and a generous benefactor to Jack B. Yeats. The couple had eight children.

Their son John (1925–92) was educated in Clongowes Wood College and the National College of Art and Design. In his book *Remembering How We Stood*, he describes Rathgar as 'clad in its reddish-brown brick, like an old russet apple or a lingering autumnal evening …' An accomplished artist, he was also a friend and benefactor to struggling writers and artists.

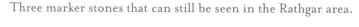

Three marker stones that can still be seen in the Rathgar area.

Marianella in its days as a private residence.

In 1954, John, along with Brian O'Nolan (Flann O'Brien), Anthony Cronin, Patrick Kavanagh and Tom Joyce, organised the first Bloomsday tour.

John bought the Bailey pub in Duke Street in 1957, and it became a haven for the Bohemian set in Dublin. John rescued the door of 7 Eccles Street, the address of Leopold Bloom in *Ulysses*, from the demolition men, and had it placed in the pub. The door is now in the James Joyce Centre, 35 North Great George's Street. John Ryan founded and edited *Envoy*, a literary and art review magazine. He chose the name *Envoy* 'to serve abroad as envoy of Irish Writing and at home as envoy of the best of international writing'. It lasted about two years, and was the first to publish Brendan Behan. John's wife, Patricia Ryan, founded the National Ballet School (1956–63).

John's sister Kathleen Ryan (1922–85) was an actress and renowned beauty. She is the subject of the painting 'The Girl in White' by Louis le Brocquy. The family later moved to Burton Hall in Leopardstown.

TODD, BURNS & CO., LIMITED
For Clerical Tailoring

WE guarantee every garment we make for fit, style and finish. We stock a huge range of Clerical cloths by the best makers, all guaranteed for colour and thoroughly shrunk.

TAILORED.				Hand Cut and Factory Finished.		
Lounge Suits	from	£5 5 0	...	£3 15 0	to	£4 15 0
Chesterfield suits	from	6 15 0	...	£5 5 0	to	£6 6 0
Tonsure	from	8 8 0	...	£6 6 0	to	£8 8 0
Frock	from	9 9 0	...	£7 10 0	to	£9 0 0
Plain Soutanes	from to	3 0 0 3 10 0	...	£2 10 0	to	£3 10 0
Slip Soutane		1 15 0 2 5 0	...	£1 7 6	to	£1 12 6
Full Roman Soutane	from to	5 0 0 6 10 0	...	Full Roman Soutane		4 10 0 5 0 0

We stock a huge range of Clerical Cloths by the Best Makers. Please write for patterns

MARY STREET - - - DUBLIN

The wide range of clerical garments available from Todd, Burns & Co.

Number 73, Ashmere, is the present headquarters of the Teachers' Union of Ireland (TUI). Ironically, two doors down was the home of John Marcus O'Sullivan, the Minister of Education who introduced the Vocational Act in 1930. In 1966, the TUI moved here from 22 North Frederick Street, purchasing the house for £15,000.

On the opposite side of Orwell Road are numbers 68, 70 and 72. The first two, St Ronan's and Abbotsford, have their names engraved in the quoin stones to the right and left of the houses. Again we see the Scottish influence. Abbotsford was occupied by William Lennan, saddler and harness manufacturer of 29 Dawson Street. Next is a house that was called Everdingen.

In front of St Ronan's is a milestone, stating 'G.P.O. 3 miles'. Before the introduction of postage stamps, the amount charged for delivery of a letter was calculated by the distance from the GPO. The mile comes from the Romans – *mile* meaning a thousand steps. In Ireland, we used to measure our miles differently from the English, but in 1824, with the foundation of the Ordnance Survey Board, we adopted the statute or English mile. The Irish mile was 2.048 kilometres, while the English or statute mile is 1.76 kilometres, so about a quarter of a mile extra.

Marianella, originally called Orwell House, was built in 1849 for William Walker Todd by Gilbert Cockburn, who of course went on to build Christ Church, Rathgar, and Zion church. William Walker Todd was a prominent businessman, owning Todd Burns and Company, drapers at 47 Mary Street. When he died in 1880, he owned property from here right down to the Dodder. Woodhurst, and then numbers 1 to 6 Orwell Park were built on his land. He also owned houses in Adelaide Road and Leinster Road.

In 1902/03, Orwell Hockey Club was run from here by the misses Mc Entaggart, who lived in the house. It was sold in 1903 to Walter Tighe, who owned the Royal Hibernian Hotel. He left for Italy, due to ill-health, and it was then occupied by George Pomeroy and his wife Edith

Marianella, a new housing development on Orwell Road, on lands previously owned by the Redemptorist Order.

Maud Olivia, who was a member of the Colley family of Corkagh House, Clondalkin. Around this time, the house's name was changed to Faunagh.

In 1916, the Redemptorist order moved into Chessington, number 30 Highfield Road. They renamed it Marianella; it is now called Hillcrest. In 1920, the Redemptorists bought Faunagh, and used it as a retreat house. They were renowned for 'fire and brimstone' retreats, which men and women had to attend separately. The fear of God was the main thrust of their teaching, very similar to the evangelical zeal of the 1850s. Of course, the major Redemptorist influence in Ireland at the beginning of the twentieth century was in 1904 in Limerick, where it is said they drove the Jews out of the city.

The original reason for the Redemptorists having a house in Rathgar was to be near a tramway or indeed within walking distance of the university for their students, which was in Earlsfort Terrace. They eventually sold the site, which has been developed into luxury apartments.

Rostrevor Terrace, off to the right, was developed in the 1860s. The walls of the field the houses overlook are a good example of the poor-quality limestone from the local quarry.

Orwell Lodge, built in 1864, is on the site of a former house called Woodhurst. In 1952, when the Corrigan family took over the house, they converted it into a hotel and called it Orwell Lodge. One of the quirks of the hotel was that never had a full bar license. It always had what was called a 'dispense bar'. The granting of a full licence depended on the number of bedrooms in the hotel, and the Orwell Lodge didn't have the required amount. Drink was served through a hatch – there was no counter. The hotel had a fine restaurant for many years.

In the 1960s, a meeting was held here, and from it Ballyboden St Enda's GAA club was formed, now one of the most successful teams in Dublin. Orwell Lodge is now an apartment complex.

Orwell Park, seen from Orwell Road. Old trees dwarf the fine houses.

Orwell Park, home
to writers John
Millington Synge,
Bram Stoker and
A.M. O'Sullivan.

ORWELL PARK

Known earlier as Dartry Park, this is a fine example of a Victorian Road. Henry Walker Todd built numbers 1 to 6 on his land. This extended down to the Dodder.

Number 4 was the home of Mrs Traill, John Millington Synge's grandmother. John Millington Synge (1871–1909) was born on 16 April 1871, in Newton Villas, Churchtown. After the death of his father, his mother decided to move to Orwell Park, to live next door to her mother, Mrs Traill. The family remained here for sixteen years, from 1872 to 1888.

The Dodder from the Rathgar side, facing Ely Arch, built by the
Ussher family in 1767 as an entrance to Rathfarnham Castle.

Synge's family were landed gentry from County Wicklow. Glanmore Castle was then their
family seat. John used to play along the Dodder and in particular in the woody demesne
of Rathfarnham Castle. The family kept a wide variety of pets, and John had a bicycle with
wooden wheels, which he cycled around the Rathgar and Churchtown area. He was always a
sickly child, and was not always let out to play. In fine weather, he would walk to Mr Harrick's
Classical and English School at 4 Upper Leeson Street. In bad weather, he would walk to

The headstone of John Millington Synge
at Mount Jerome Cemetery.

Rathgar and get the tram. With the proximity of the Dodder, Synge developed a passionate interest in nature, and joined the Dublin Naturalists' Field Club in the mid-1880s. He also kept wild animals in the back garden of the house.

Synge went to his father's family estate in County Wicklow for his holidays. He was a musician before he became a playwright, studying piano, flute and violin. In 1891, he won a scholarship in counterpoint at the Royal Irish Academy of Music. Following a trip to Germany in 1892, he decided that his talents lay in literature rather than music. However, his musical ability was to prove very useful when he went to the Aran Islands, where he was accepted by the islanders, who appreciated his fine fiddle playing. He absorbed their culture and, under the influence of W.B. Yeats, who told him to 'express a life that has never found expression', he wrote *The Playboy of the Western World*. It is well known that the play caused a riot when it was first performed on 26 January 1907.

In later life, Synge came back to south Dublin, and lived in various flats. These included 15 Maxwell Road, Rathmines; 57 Rathgar Road; and 47 York Road, Rathmines. He died on 24 March 1909, in the Elpis Nursing Home, Lower Mount Street, and is buried in Mount Jerome Cemetery, Harold's Cross. He wrote his own epitaph, part of which reads:

A silent sinner, nights and days
No human heart to him drew nigh,
Alone he wound his wonted ways.
Alone and little loved did die.

Mr and Mrs Abraham Stoker, parents of Abraham or Bram Stoker, author of *Dracula*, also lived in number 4, from 1865 to 1869.

The Stokers moved to this house because they could not afford to keep their house at 15 Marino Crescent, Clontarf, where Bram (1847–1912) was born. When Abraham senior retired, they moved to Rathgar. It was during these years that Bram was at Trinity College. Bram probably didn't live here, but he obviously would have visited.

Bram's mother, Charlotte Thornley, was reared in Sligo, where she would have seen the devastation and death wrought by the cholera epidemic of the 1820s, and the poverty and utter desolation of the west of Ireland at that time. Her tales of the cholera outbreak are widely regarded as the basis for Bram's most famous story, *Dracula*. In Charlotte's account in her journal, terrible deeds are done: A traveller is buried alive. The God-fearing Protestants believe the famine is a punishment from God for Catholics, so the papists are treated as plague carriers. One image she recounts is of a Roman Catholic priest, armed with a horsewhip, protecting bodies to prevent them from being carried out before they are dead. Bram was influenced by these horrific stories.

His father, also Abraham, was a government official. He was forty-four when he married Charlotte, who was twenty-five. Although there may have been a large age difference between them, Charlotte was no 'shrinking violet'. She was heavily influenced by the Bible and wrote several papers on a wide variety of topics. *Female Emigration for Workhouses* was published in 1864.

Among her famous phrases was: 'What is our whole system of female education but a matrimonial speculation?' Having travelled around Europe, she ended her days back at 72 Rathgar

Road, and died in 1901. She had spent about fifteen years there, and regularly attended Rathfarnham Church of Ireland parish church, where there is a memorial to the Stoker family. Charlotte and her husband are buried in Mount Jerome cemetery.

Around the time that his parents moved to Orwell Park, Bram entered Trinity College. Though he had been a sickly child, he excelled as an adult on the sports field. His greatest achievement

Abraham 'Bram' Stoker.

was winning the 'Overall Champion' of the Trinity Sports in 1867. He was a good rugby player and a gymnast. Standish O'Grady, the historian and novelist, played with him. Bram was Auditor of the Trinity College

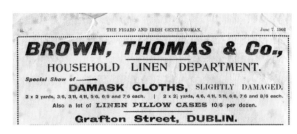

Historical Society, the world's oldest student society. Not surprisingly, with all these activities, he took six years to complete a four-year BA course. After five years, he bought his master's degree, a practice that can be done to this day.

Having met Henry Irvine, Bram went to manage the Lyceum theatre for him in London. He married Florence Balcombe in 1878. Florence had been seeing Oscar Wilde, and indeed Oscar felt jilted and demanded a worthless gold cross back that he had given her the previous Christmas.

Alexander Mark O'Sullivan K.C. (1871–1959) also lived in number 4. He received the title 'Third King's Sergeant' in 1912, then Second, and finally First King's Sergeant in 1921; the last man to hold the title. Alexander was on the legal team that defended Roger Casement.

The entrance gates to Oaklands, now St Luke's Hospital, Orwell Park.
The initials CWH on the gates stand for Charles Wisdom Hely.

He left a vivid account of the experience, describing how he had a dreadful attack of nerves and remembered little of the proceedings. He felt he had disgraced himself. He was a constitutional nationalist, and opposed Sinn Féin. He opposed conscription, but felt there was a need to help the Irishmen at the front line.

O'Sullivan was seen as part of the establishment, becoming Chairman of the Irish Recruiting Council. He survived several attempts on his life, and finally, in 1921, he and his family fled to England. He returned to Ireland in 1950. He wrote two books: *Old Ireland Reminiscences of an Irish K.C.* (1927) and *The Last Sergeant* (1952), written very much from a Catholic establishment point of view. The former gives a little-heard perspective on our quest for Irish independence.

Number 58, Lisnoe, was the home of John Hamilton Reid, Chairman of Switzer & Co. from 1892 to 1907. Switzer & Co. was a prestigious shop on Grafton Street, where Brown Thomas is located now.

Number 13, Oaklands (back gate). On the gates is the monogram C.W.H. – Charles Wisdom Hely of Hely Thoms, printers and stationers.

Opposite: Dartry House, off Orwell Park, was the
home of industrialist William Martin Murphy.
Above: Author Ged Walsh standing between the
original gate piers of Dartry House.
Right: Dartry House, with its distinctive tower.

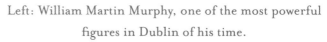

Left: William Martin Murphy, one of the most powerful
figures in Dublin of his time.
Below left: His son, Dr William Lombard Murphy, surgeon,
linguist and diplomat.

Orwell Bank was the manse of Christ Church, Rathgar,
occupied by Reverend Stevenson. The Church sold it in 1898
to another Presbyterian, James Adams, whose auctioneering
business was located in St Stephen's Green. It is still there
today. Adams was a member of the Board of the Rathmines
and Rathgar Township, and also Governor of the Royal Hospital,
Donnybrook.

Number 23, Minore, was the residence of George Beater (1850–1928).
An architect with an extensive practice, among his designs were the Arnotts
shop in Henry Street and the Featherstonehaugh Convalescent Home
for the Adelaide Hospital in Braemor Park. His father lived in Gle-
narm on Terenure Road East, and was Chairman of Arnotts.

Dartry House was originally built by James Drury, another
prominent Presbyterian who lived in the house.

He was followed by William Martin Murphy. There were few
people in Dublin at that time more prestigious than William
Martin Murphy. He was among the most influential businessmen in the city, owning the Dublin United Tramways Company,
Independent Newspapers and Clery's department store. Nor did he
restrict his business interests to Ireland – he travelled to various parts
of the world, and built railways in England, South America and on the
Gold Coast of West Africa.

Originally from Bantry, County Cork, the Murphy family moved to
Dublin and William was educated at Belvedere College. On the death
of his father, he took over the family building business aged nineteen.

Right: The clubhouse at Milltown Golf Club,
built in 1907 and burnt down in 1959.
Below right: A beautiful tribute to James
Drury, who built Dartry House.

He was elected a nationalist Member of Parliament for St Patrick's Ward, Dublin, from
1885 to 1892. Although disillusioned with
nationalist politics, he refused a knighthood
from King Edward VII in 1906. Murphy
was President of Milltown Golf Club from
1907 until his death in 1919.

Of course, he is best remembered for
leading the employers of Dublin against the
trade unions in the confrontation that led
to the Dublin lock-out of 1913. His son,
Dr William Lombard Murphy (Lombard
coming from his mother's maiden name),
was an ear, nose and throat surgeon at St
Vincent's Hospital, and served as a member
of the Royal Army Medical Corps during
the First World War. Being a linguist and
stationed in Salonika, William became a

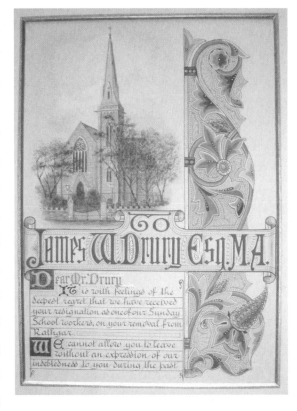

liaison officer between British, French and Serbian medical units. Among his awards were
Le Croix de Guerre, the Chevalier of the Legion of Honour, the Serbian Order of St Sava
and the Greek Order of the Redeemer.

William represented Saorstát Éireann at the 1929 and 1930 International Labour Conferences
in Geneva. He continued his father's business interests, and was also a patron of the Feis Ceol and
the Rathmines & Rathgar Musical Society. On his death in 1943, he left an estate of £150,000,
which included a legacy to Dr Oliver Chance, a pioneering cancer specialist.

There was a raid on the house on 27 February 1923, during the Civil War, with the IRA attempting to enter at gunpoint. Dr Murphy, unfazed, went upstairs and rang a bell out the bedroom window to alert the police. The raiders ran off, leaving canisters of petrol behind.

The house and lands were acquired by the Mill Hill Fathers in the early 1960s. They have gradually sold off the land, and the house is now in apartments.

ORWELL ROAD

Belford is on the hill down to the Dodder. Tommy Webster, a local Quaker historian, lived there for forty years and he always maintained that the name was significant. He said that before a bridge was built over the Dodder, a bell was rung from this house if someone was fording the river. The ford was located further downstream.

Orwell House, originally the home of Patrick Waldron, which has also served as the Bethany Home for pregnant unmarried Church of Ireland girls. It is now Orwell House nursing home.

Beside the Dodder on Orwell Road. The house on the right is an old building associated with William Carvill's water-powered sawmill, while the one on the left is more recent.

Rathgar House, now called **Orwell House**, was the home of Patrick Waldron (1772–1851). He built this house in 1830, which was unusual at the time, as not many Roman Catholics had the means to do so. He had a business at Inns Quay, called Waldron, Osbrey and Waldron. Mr Osbrey also lived in Rathgar.

In the 1830s, Waldron formed Waldron, Dodd, Carton & Co., a calico and muslin bleaching and printing business. The factory, located just below the house, employed 300 people at its height. The works were powered by a water mill, which was located here since the eighteenth century and was known as the 'Lord Chief Justice's Mill'. When Patrick took over the premises, he installed a new water mill. The millrace flowed around where the High School's hockey pitch is now and then back to the Dodder, at the bridge.

At this time, there were several calico printing works in Dublin, such as at Islandbridge, Ballsbridge, Palmerstown and Crumlin, as well as in the north of Ireland. There was an extensive calico printing works in Stratford on Slaney, County Wicklow. Calico, a light, cotton fabric, was imported generally from India. When it arrived, it was first bleached. This used an enormous amount of water. After bleaching came the printing process. This was labour-intensive, as the fabric was placed on boards and block-printed. The more simple printing was often blue and white. However, often up to nine colours were used, each colour applied separately. The calico printing industry effectively ceased in the 1850s.

When Patrick died in 1851, he left £11,000 and an instruction to build a bridge over the Dodder. He also owned the land at the east side of the river. The bridge was known as Waldron's Bridge for years. He is buried in St Nahi's graveyard, Dundrum.

William Carvill now purchased the house and mill. With his partner, Joseph Meade, he ran a sawmill here until 1895.

The Egan sisters lived in the house, followed by Joseph Walker, a dentist. In 1936, it became the Bethany Home, a home for Protestant unmarried mothers. It was taken over in 1970 by the Girls' Friendly Society, and became a hostel for Protestant girls who were working in the city. It is now Orwell Nursing Home.

The Dodder Anglers' Association was formed in 1958. Among the founders were William Boyd Fawcett (first President), who drew up the first rules, Hughie Nolan (first Chairman) and Rory Harkin (first Treasurer). The biggest anglers' club in the country, it currently has a membership of 1,200. Each year, the members stock the river for the start of the fishing season, 17 March. They make great efforts to police the environment in the surrounding Dodder catchment area.

The late Paddy Conneff, who joined in the first year, was a renowned angler. He told the story of how, when he was a boy fishing below Orwell Weir, there was a house situated to the right with no sanitation, above the weir. The woman who lived there used to come out and throw tea leaves and worse indiscriminately into the river, and God help anybody fishing beneath the weir.

Beside the weir is one of the marking stones indicating the edge of the Rathmines Township.

RATHGAR VILLAGE

The crossroads at Rathgar village is the meeting point of Orwell Road, Terenure Road East, Rathgar Avenue, Rathgar Road and Highfield Road.

RATHGAR ROAD

This was the new Rathgar Road, dating from about 1804. In the early almanacs, there are only a dozen or so listings for this road, most of them at the Rathmines end. It wasn't until the formation of the Rathmines Township in 1847 that the road started to be developed. It was built in a ribbon development pattern, with builders buying sites for terraces of houses.

As you can see, they are fairly common in appearance – three storeys, with pillared main doorways and steps up to the hall door. At ground level there is another door, used for servants and deliveries.

The southeastern corner of Rathgar crossroads, showing SuperValu, Bijou restaurant, the old Gourmet shop, Bijou deli, Bracken estate agents, the ex-Organic Supermarket and MacDonald's cycles.

Number 98A Rathgar Road, site of a raid on an IRA arms cache.

The ground-floor walls were often built from the local limestone, and because of its poor quality, they were plastered over. Notice the railings at the front between each house in the terrace. The road used to be known by each terrace, but from 1866 on, it was continuously numbered, for ease of delivery of post and so on. However, for many years the locals refused to change, and kept referring to the old names.

IRA Raid at Boyne Stores: 98A Rathgar Road

On 16 August 1940, Gardaí raided a small grocery store at 98A Rathgar Road, owned by William Ryan and believed to be an IRA training centre. Garda Richard Hyland and Sergeant Patrick Mc Keown, in the vanguard, received a volley of shots and were killed as they tried to enter the shop by the front door. Detective Pat Brady was also seriously wounded.

Three IRA men – Patrick McGrath, Tommy Harte and Tom Hunt – burst out through the door and ran down the street. Harte was shot in the leg as he ran away towards Wesley Road. A Thomson machine gun was thrown into a garden on Wesley Road. Gardaí took McGrath and Harte prisoner at 20 Wesley Road, where the wounded raider was attended to and they were given tea and biscuits. Tom Hunt evaded the Gardaí until he was caught on 22 August.

A large quantity of ammunition and many revolvers were found in the shop, as well as a number of dry batteries and other wireless parts. The shop was scarred with bullet holes, with seventeen holes in the right front window.

The men were charged under the new Military Court established by the Emergency Powers Act of 1939. After hearing all of the evidence, the court adjourned for fifteen minutes, and found the defendants guilty. Two days later, the Government ratified the judgement and ordered the prisoners to be shot. An appeal went to the Supreme Court, but it was dismissed.

Patrick McGrath and Tommy Harte were executed by firing squad in Mountjoy Prison at 6.45pm on 6 September 1940. Tom Hunt's death sentence was commuted to penal servitude for life.

This episode was part of the aftermath of an IRA raid, in which they had stolen the entire stock of ammunition kept in the Magazine Fort in Phoenix Park. This was the reason the Military Court was set up. Patrick McGrath had been a hunger striker in 1939, and had been released by Éamon de Valera.

Rosair now has four houses. This was the residence of Seamus Fenning, a bookseller in Dawson Street and Irish billiards champion. He had the distinction of appearing in the 1937 Oliver St John Gogarty libel case, when the doctor was sensationally accused of libelling a Jewish man named Harry Sinclair in a satirical verse included in his *As I Was Going Down Sackville Street*. Another witness in that case was Samuel Beckett. Although he was not the author of the verse, Gogarty lost the case, and became very disillusioned with Ireland.

WINTON AVENUE

This avenue was built around 1864. It is named after Archibald W. Montgomery, 13th Earl of Eglinton and Winton (1821–61).

Number 70 Rathgar Road was the home of Dr James Drumm (1897–1974). This is the man we have to thank when we recharge our mobile phones. Having graduated from UCD in 1924, he worked on developing his alkaline nickel/zinc rechargeable battery in the UCD labs in Merrion Street between 1926 and 1931. It was called the Drumm Traction Battery, and at the time was regarded as the best battery ever invented, as it could be recharged more quickly than acid batteries. It was installed and tested

Dr James Drumm.

on a train from Dublin to Portarlington, a distance of eighty miles, which it managed on a single charge. Then it was used regularly on the Dublin–Bray railway line from 1932 to 1948.

However, it was soon felt that diesel was more efficient and readily available, and the battery was discontinued. When we see the many uses of rechargeable batteries in modern technology, Dr Drumm seems to have been a man way ahead of his time.

Number 60 housed the sculptor Joseph Robinson Kirk, RHA (1821–94), son of the noted Cork-born sculptor Thomas Kirk (1781–1845). Continuing the family tradition, Joseph executed several sculptures. He was most noted for his portrait busts. His public works include the four figures of the Campanile in Trinity College: Divinity, Law, Medicine and Science; and the statues of St Peter and St Patrick on St Paul's Church, Arran Quay. He later moved to Milward Terrace, Bray, where he died. He is buried in Mount Jerome Cemetery, Harold's Cross.

Number 53 was the home of Dr Seamus O'Kelly (1881–1918) and his wife in 1916. This house had a significant part in the history of Ireland. A meeting was held here on Easter Saturday, 22 April 1916, in which it was decided to countermand the order for the Rising.

Pádraic Pearse met Eoin MacNeill on Holy Thursday night, 1916, MacNeill asking what they should do about the 'Castle Document'. Eoin MacNeill was unaware that the Rising had been planned for Easter Sunday, although he was Chairman of the Irish Volunteers. Pearse told MacNeill, 'We have used you and your name and influence for what it was worth. You can issue what orders you like now, our men won't obey you.'

Number 53 Rathgar Road, where the historic meeting took place on the Saturday before the 1916 Rising.

The Rebellion had been arranged for Easter Sunday. On Easter Saturday morning, the newspapers carried a report of the capture and arrest of an unknown stranger on Banna Strand in Kerry. This was in fact Roger Casement, but he was not identified at the time. The arms intended for Rising sank with the scuttling of the ship *Aud* off the Cork coast.

Eoin MacNeill called the meeting in Dr O'Kelly's house on Saturday night. It was attended by Eoin Mac Neill, Seamus O'Kelly, The O'Rahilly, Arthur Griffith, Sean T. O'Kelly, Sean Fitzgibbon, Dr James Ryan, Miss Min Ryan, Colm Ó Lochlainn, Paudeen O'Keeffe and Liam O'Brian. Three leaders of the Rising – Pearse, MacDonagh and Plunkett – called to the house to persuade MacNeill to let it go ahead. MacNeill felt it couldn't succeed, and would only cause more bloodshed. One witness that evening stated that there was almost a traffic jam outside the house, with all the comings and goings. There were heated arguments for and against the Rising going ahead.

" Owing to the very critical position, all orders given to Irish Volunteers for to-morrow, Easter Sunday, are hereby rescinded, and no parades, marches, or other movements of Irish Volunteers will take place. Each individual Volunteer will obey this order strictly in every particular."

Above right: The order to stand down, printed in the *Sunday Independent* on the morning the Rising was originally intended to take place.

Right: Colm O Lochlainn's the Sign of the Three Candles at Fleet Street.

97

Number 158 Rathgar Road, previously the home of republican activist Colm Ó Lochlainn,
publisher with the Sign of the Three Candles press.

It was from this meeting that the order cancelling the Rising was issued. Eoin cycled from the
house to the *Sunday Independent* offices in Abbey Street to have the notice printed in the paper.
Other people at the meeting travelled to various other parts of the country cancelling the Rising.
This led to enormous confusion, not only in Dublin but in the rest of Ireland also.

The Military Council of the IRB met and decided to accede to MacNeill's orders. Meanwhile,
the organisers of the Rising held a meeting and decided to go ahead with the Rising, one day late,
at noon on Easter Monday.

Number 158, Beechlawn, was the home of Colm Ó Lochlainn (1892–1972), who established
the Sign of The Three Candles press – the 'three candles' being Truth, Nature (Wisdom) and
Knowledge. His father lived here and worked at the printing firm of Ó Lochlainn, Murphy and
Boland of Upper Dorset Street.

Having attended Belvedere College and St Mary's College, Ó Lochlainn graduated from
UCD in 1914. He received his MA in 1916. One of his lecturers in UCD was Eoin MacNeill.
He became an assistant teacher in St Enda's School, Rathfarnham.

Ó Lochlainn was on the executive of the Irish Volunteers. On Good Friday of Easter week 1916, he and several others were told to go to Cahersiveen to dismantle the radio station there and bring the sets back to Dublin. Having taken the train to Killarney, the team then travelled in two cars. Ó Lochlainn travelled in the first car with Denis Daly, with Sam Windrim as the driver. The second car had Tommy McInerney as driver and Con Keating, Daniel Sheehan and Charlie Monahan as passengers. The cars were meant to be in convoy, but they became separated. The second car took a wrong turn at Killorglin and plunged into a river, drowning three of its occupants. These men could be regarded as the first casualties of the 1916 Rising. Tommy McInerney was the only survivor. Ó Lochlainn and Denis Daly returned to Dublin empty-handed.

Ó Lochlainn took part in the meeting at 53 Rathgar Road on that Saturday night. He was dispatched to Dundalk and Coalisland with the news that the Rising was cancelled. His printing skills were put to good use during that time. He also printed the receipts for the Government bonds issued in 1919 to help fund the War of Independence.

Ó Lochlainn was an uilleann pipe player and a noted collector of ballads. He published *Irish Street Ballads* (1939) and *More Irish Street Ballads* (1965), using distinctive type fonts that he designed himself. He was a lecturer in Irish language and literature at UCD from 1933 to 1943. In 1931, he also found time to be one of the founders of An Óige. His sons and daughter carried on the family tradition in music. He is buried in Glasnevin Cemetery.

Pádraic Pearse used the Three Candles sign over the door of his first school, Cullenswood House on Oakley Road.

FRANKFORT AVENUE

Frankfort Avenue (1843) was named after Raymond Harvey de Montmorency, Right Honourable Baron Frankfort (1835–1902), who was a major landlord in the area.

Number 1, St Mary's, was the home of Count and Countess Markievicz in 1904/05, before they moved to Surrey House on Leinster Road. The Countess was born Constance Gore-Booth in 1868 in London. The family had estates in Lissadell, County Sligo. Constance studied painting at the Slade School of Art in London. She then went to Paris and met fellow student

Number 1 Frankfort Avenue, the home of Countess Constance Markievicz, republican revolutionary, the first woman elected to the British Parliament, and Minister for Labour in the Free State Parliament.

Count Casimir Dunin-Markievicz, a Catholic from Polish landed stock. Six years her junior, he had been married before and had two sons. His wife died in 1899.

Constance and the Count married in London in 1900. Their only child, Maeve Allys, was born in Lissadell in November 1901, and was raised by her grandmother, Lady Georgina Gore-Booth. Maeve was educated in England, and spent most of her life there, returning to Sligo for holidays. She died in London in 1962.

Constance and Casimir moved to Dublin in 1903. Fired up with the spirit of Irish nationalism, Constance co-founded Na Fianna Éireann, a training organisation for young nationalist boys. They were taught drill, the use of firearms and first aid.

The Countess ran a soup kitchen with Inghinidhe na hÉireann for the workers of the General Strike in 1913, and became a member of the Irish Citizen Army in 1914. During the 1916 Rising, she was second in command to Michael Mallin at the Royal College of Surgeons in St Stephen's Green.

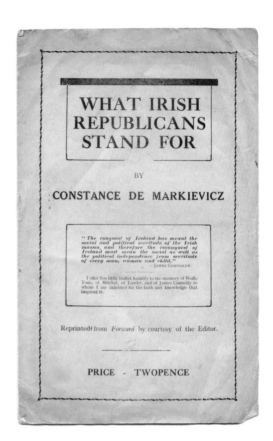

Countess Markievicz, and a political pamphlet she produced.

After the Rising, Constance was arrested and sentenced to death, though this was commuted to penal servitude. She was released in 1917, and became a Catholic convert, taking the baptismal name Anastasia. She also performed in the newly founded Abbey Theatre. As a Sinn Féin candidate in the general election of 1918, she became the first woman to be elected to the British House of Commons, although she didn't take her seat, in line with the Sinn Féin policy of the time.

When Éamon de Valera set up the Provisional Government in 1919, the Countess was Minister for Labour, the only female cabinet minister. The next female minister was Máire Geoghegan-Quinn, Minister for the Gaeltacht from 1977. Markievicz was strongly anti-Treaty, and in 1923 she went on hunger strike. She joined Fianna Fáil on its foundation in 1926. She died on 15 July 1927. Casimir, who had returned to Poland in 1913, came back for the funeral. Constance is buried in the Republican plot in Glasnevin cemetery.

Historian George Little, who lived at number 28.

In the 1950s, there was a proposal that the Portobello Barracks in Rathmines should be renamed in her honour, but the minister of the time rejected the proposal, on the grounds that the ordinary people of Dublin would not be able to spell Markievicz! It was instead renamed Cathal Brugha Barracks.

Incredibly, the only statue commemorating a historic female in Dublin is that of Countess Markievicz, in St Stephen's Green.

Number 26, Westan, was the residence of William Beale Jacob and his wife Hanna in the 1860s. They were members of the Religious Society of Friends (Quakers). William and his brother Robert had come from Waterford to Dublin to expand their business. With the help of Samuel Bewley and Charles Bewley Pim (fellow Quakers), they set up business in June 1861, founding the company W. & R. Jacob, in Peter's Row. The property extended to 'Big Butter Lane', also known as Bishop Street. Robert Jacob married Hanna Walpole, and they lived in Garville Villa.

Robert took frequent holidays with Hanna's brother James. On Sunday, 13 October 1861, while on holiday in Tramore, County Waterford, Robert and James went for a walk before dinner. Sadly, they were never to be seen again. Robert's body was found at the foot of the cliffs near the statue of the 'Metal Man'. James's body was found three days later. Although Robert was only involved in the company for the first few years, William kept his brother's initial in the name.

Number 28 housed a large medical practice run by Dr George A. Little, a doctor and medical officer of the old IRA. His other great passion was local history. He was among the first to join the Old Dublin Society, and was its President in 1942. He read over fourteen papers to the society, arranged numerous outings and was very much involved in establishing a Civic Museum for Dublin. Sadly we no longer have one. Dr Little wrote *Dublin before the Vikings* and *Malachi Horan Remembers*. The latter is a gem of the folklore of the Dublin Mountains, told to him by the said Malachi Horan, who lived in Killenarden, Tallaght.

George's eccentric brother, Francis, lived with him. In the 1920s, Francis took a very public stand against the decline of morals. He covered his clothes with a sack, and waged war against silk stockings and low necklines. While travelling by tram, if he noticed a lady with what he considered a revealing neckline, he would offer her a handkerchief, and if she refused to use it, he would exhort the men on the tram to leave. He was well known in Rathgar and Rathmines.

Number 18 was owned by May Langan, and later by a Mr Kilbride. It was here that Erskine Childers ran his Ministry of Propaganda. Lily (Elizabeth) O'Brennan (1848–1948) was a sister of Áine Ceannt, the wife of Éamonn Ceannt, one of the signatories of the 1916 Proclamation. Lily was also a committed republican. During the Rising, she was with the Marrowbone Lane garrison. She served as a District Judge in the Republican Courts during the War of Independence. Lily went on to become Arthur Griffith's secretary during the Treaty negotiations. She opposed the Treaty, and became secretary to Erskine Childers.

Number 36 Rathgar Avenue, opposite Kenilworth Square South. One of the oldest houses on the road, dating from 1851, this was built as a hunting lodge, and is named Eagle Lodge.

Number 99c was where one of the first bookies shops was located, now the Butler's Pantry. It was owned by Joe Cunningham, whose family owned Shamrock Rovers Football Club. Bookmakers, or turf accountants as they used to be called, first appeared in Ireland after the Betting Act of 1926, which regulated gambling and granted licences to bookmakers.

RATHGAR AVENUE

Number 1 is now incorporated into Comans pub. The novelist William Carleton (1794–1869) lived here. Born in County Tyrone, when he arrived in Dublin he earned his living as a tutor. He wrote *Traits and Stories of the Irish Peasantry* in 1830, and it quickly went on to several editions. The Land War and Irish peasantry featured in a lot of his works. When he died he was living at Woodville on Sandford Road, Ranelagh. He is buried in Mount Jerome Cemetery in Harold's Cross.

3a, Halcyon Cottage, is now a large house called **Fairfield House**. Susan Mitchell (1866–1926) lived here from 1923 to 1926. She had previously lived in a number of addresses around Rathgar and Rathmines, most notably 16 Frankfurt Avenue. She was born in the Provincial Bank building in Carrick on Shannon, County Leitrim. When her father died, she came to live with her two aunts in Dublin. She was sent to London in 1900, and stayed with the Yeats family. In 1901, she became assistant editor of *Irish Homestead* magazine, edited by George Russell (A.E.). Her book *Aids to the Immortality of Certain Persons* is a satirical look at her contemporaries in literature and public life. She was a prominent member of the United Arts Club, and a renowned hostess.

HARRISON ROW

Airfield House was the home of Mr Jordan, a road contractor who owned Rathgar Quarry. Airfield Terrace was built on the land of Airfield House around 1863, and Airfield Road was built around 1910 on the lands of this house.

AIRFIELD ROAD

As you turn into Airfield Road (1912), on your right-hand side there is a sign on the side of the house: 'Jehovah – Jireh – the Lord will provide'. Apparently one of the previous owners of the house ran into financial difficulties, and was in despair. Then out of the blue, he was bequeathed a legacy, which solved his money problems. He put the sign up as a message of thanksgiving.

Number 8 has a plaque to Francis and Hanna Sheehy-Skeffington. They lived there before moving to Grosvenor Road.

Number 16 was regarded by Michael Collins as one of the two safest houses in Dublin in which to hide. It is said that he ate his dinner here after the events of Bloody Sunday.

Rathgar Boys' and Girls' National School is halfway down Rathgar Avenue. It was founded as a Methodist junior school in 1896. The Hamilton family owned land here, and also on the north side of Winton Avenue. The Methodist church opened in 1874 on Brighton Road, but the school was built on Rathgar Avenue, not next door to the church, as there was not enough space. Built to accommodate 160 pupils, it cost £640, of which a grant of £426.13.4 was made available from the Commissioners of National Education. It was opened on 4 August 1896, and then the boys' and girls' schools merged in 1970.

Winton Avenue beside the school takes its name from Winton Villa, and connects with Rathgar Road.

COULSON AVENUE (1885)

Number 26 was the first home of Maud Gonne and John MacBride, from 1905. Their baby was born in France, but they wanted the christening to be in Ireland. Seagan (John, Joannes) Gonne MacBride was christened in St Joseph's church, Terenure. His grandmother, Honoria MacBride,

Hanna and her son Owen Sheehy-Skeffington.

Rathgar National School on Rathgar Avenue.

was godmother. There is no godfather listed, because the parish priest, Canon Terence Anderson, objected to John O'Leary standing as godfather, as he was a well-known agnostic. The child became known as Seán MacBride.

Maud Gonne was born in 1866. Her father was a colonel in the British Army. She and her young sister Kathleen went to Paris, where Maud Gonne met and fell in love with a Frenchman called Lucien Millevoye. They had two children: George, born in 1891, and Iseult, born in 1894. George died in infancy. The couple separated about 1900. Maud Gonne was able to finance herself from a legacy left to her by her mother.

John MacBride was born in 1865 in Westport. He came to Dublin to find work, and signed up with the Irish Brigade in the Boer War in South Africa. When the Irish Brigade disbanded in 1900, he went to Paris, and there he met Maud. She was a beautiful, sophisticated, European woman. Their family and friends advised against marriage, especially Arthur Griffith, who begged them not to marry. However, the wedding went ahead in 1904. Maud converted to Catholicism before her marriage, and had all the zeal of a convert. By the time they moved to Rathgar, however, the marriage was already in trouble. In 1905, Maud sued for divorce and got a judicial separation.

Maud wanted to bar John from visiting her son in her Parisian home. His access was limited to two hours every Monday afternoon. John decided to return to Dublin, and had no more contact with them. Maud only spoke French to the boy, so that if John did return, he would not be able to communicate with him.

The divorce case was a *cause célèbre* in all the Irish papers, except for one. The *United Irishman*, Arthur Griffith's paper, didn't report on it at all. Censorship has many forms.

It is widely known that W.B. Yeats had been attracted to Maud for ten years prior to her wedding. To complicate matters further, Maud Gonne's father had an illegitimate daughter called Eileen Wilson, who married Joseph MacBride, John's older brother.

When John MacBride was executed following the 1916 Rising, Maud thought that the rebels would be heroes, so she returned to Dublin. Meanwhile, she spurned W.B. Yeats's affections. Maud now called herself Madame Gonne-MacBride. She joined Sinn Féin, and was imprisoned in Holloway Prison with Countess Markievicz. She often wore a veil falling from head to below knee.

It was around this time that she learned of the death of Lucien Millevoye, and also that of her sister Kathleen.

Back in Dublin, Maud and Seán lived at 73 St Stephen's Green. Seán MacBride joined the IRA in 1919, although he was only fifteen at the time. In 1920, Iseult ran off with another boy to England. Of course this boy would become the poet Francis Stuart. Maud and Francis never had a good relationship.

After the War of Independence, Seán was present at the Treaty negotiations, in his role as bodyguard to Michael Collins. Now within the family there was another split, after the Treaty had been signed. Maud was in favour, regarding it as a stepping-stone towards independence. Seán opposed it strongly.

Maud Gonne-MacBride published an autobiography called *Servant of the Queen* in 1948. She died in April 1953, and Seán died in January 1987, both at Roebuck House, Clonskeagh.

Seán had married Catalina 'Kid' Bulfin (1901–76), daughter of the well-known nationalist and writer William Bulfin. He was survived by his son Tiernan (1932–95) and daughter Anna Mac-Bride-White (1927–2011).

Number 17 Rathgar Avenue has a plaque on the wall to indicate that this was the home of George William Russell between 1911 and 1933. Before that, between 1900 and 1905, the Russells lived in Coulson Avenue. George was always known as A.E., and the way he acquired the nickname is interesting. He submitted an article for publication that he signed AEON, but his writing was so illegible that the printer couldn't make it out, so he just put down AE.

Born in Lurgan in County Armagh, he moved to Dublin and was educated in Rathmines, and then worked as a clerk in Pim's, a drapery store in George's Street. He attended the Metropolitan School of Art, where he met fellow student W.B. Yeats.

Russell got involved in the co-operative movement in 1889 with Sir Horace Plunkett. In 1894, the Irish Agriculture Organisation Society was set up, and he became heavily involved. He travelled around Ireland on a bike and became editor of its paper, *The Irish Homestead*.

Number 17 Rathgar Avenue. The plaque beside the door identifies this as the home of George Russell, 'A.E.', painter, writer, revolutionary and founder of the Irish cooperative movement.

Number 26 Coulson Avenue, the first home
of Maud Gonne and John MacBride.

In 1904, he published James Joyce's short stories 'Eveline' and 'The Sisters', published under the name Stephen Dedalus.

A.E. became noted as a writer and publisher. His first collection of poems was called *Homeward: Songs by the Way* (1894). He was greatly interested in theosophy – the idea of divine inspiration driving specially gifted people, as well as abnormal control over natural forces.

Russell used to a have an 'at home' every Sunday evening, and was encouraging and kind to everyone, but in particular young authors. The author George Moore said of him, 'He settles everybody's difficulties and consoles the afflicted.' The children of the area called him 'the hairy fairy' because of his long beard.

He was prolific in his output. In addition to writing, he painted extremely well, producing at least 400 paintings. After the death of his wife in 1932, A.E. went to live in England, and died in Bournemouth in 1935. His body was brought back to Dublin for burial in Mount Jerome Cemetery.

BRIGHTON SQUARE (1864)

This road was previously known as Cromwell Road, and then became Kensington Road. The whole Brighton Square area was built for people of the Methodist faith. When the houses were advertised, it was stated that a church was convenient to all who purchased a house here.

It is strange that Brighton Square has only three sides: south, east and west. I suppose calling it Brighton Triangle wouldn't sound right. The houses surround a green area with tennis courts and football pitches. For quite a while, the tennis club was for residents' use only, but eventually it was opened to outsiders. The William Spence Memorial, 1903, is over the clubhouse. Spence had a huge steel and armaments factory in Cork Street, covering about three or four acres. He supplied armaments to the British government for the First World War.

Numbers 67 and 68 have big steel vases of fruit in front of them, with Spence's name on them. He lived in one of these houses, built in the 1870s. There is also a street off Cork Street named after his wife. Following the 1916 Rising, he felt it was unsafe to continue living here, particularly as he was an arms manufacturer for the British government, so he went to England.

Number 41 was the birthplace of James Joyce, on 2 February 1882. Indicative of their future lifestyle, the Joyce family only lived here for a couple of years, before moving to 23 Castlewood Avenue, and then on and on to several more addresses.

Joyce's parents met in the choir of the Church of the Three Patrons, Rathgar. Their first home was 13 Ontario Terrace, Rathmines, and James was baptised in St Joseph's Church in Terenure.

James Joyce only mentions Rathgar briefly in *Ulysses*. But he does set the party where Molly first meets Leopold Bloom in Mat Dillon's house, Brighton House, 11 Brighton Road, Roundtown. Roundtown was the old name for Terenure, changed in 1868.

Before Joyce became an industry, an American professor, Dr Fredric Young, a minister, poet and teacher, convinced his students at Montclair State University, New Jersey, to raise funds for a plaque for this house. It was unveiled on 16 June 1964.

Number 43 was home to David Comyn (1854–1907), a man who had a significant influence on the Irish language. He was co-founder of the Society for the Preservation of the Irish Language

in 1876. He wrote *Irish Illustrations to Shakespeare* (1894), and his book *The Youthful Exploits of Fionn* is said to have had a major influence on W.B. Yeats.

The steel vases at numbers 67 and 68 Brighton Square.

BRIGHTON ROAD

Just before you get to the top of Brighton Road, there is Tower Avenue, named after the water tower that once stood here. In the 1870s, when the new water supply was organised by the Rathmines and Rathgar Township, the supply did not reach the whole area. The tower built here was sixty feet above the highest house in Rathgar, and held about 100,000 gallons.

Number 41 Brighton Square, the birthplace
of James Joyce. Can you spot his ghost?

TERENURE ROAD EAST

Two items are worth noting on this road – another milestone: '3 miles G.P.O.'; and a boundary stone, marking the edge of the Rathmines and Rathgar Township.

Terenure Road East was built at the beginning of the eighteenth century, and was originally known as Terenure Road. Its large houses were built in the same ribbon-development fashion as Rathgar Road. Coman's pub and restaurant is located on the corner of Terenure Road East and Rathgar Avenue.

Until the late 1940s, the Munster and Leinster Bank in Rathgar, which opened in 1910, was located just opposite where AIB is now. You can see the faded sign above the Bottler's Bank pub. The Munster and Leinster Bank amalgamated with the Provincial and Royal Banks in 1966, to form the Allied Irish Banks group. The sign on the side of Coman's, which says 'established in 1847', relates to the business, not the pub itself. Coman's was, at that time, a wine and spirit merchant.

Rathgar village from Terenure Road East, showing Bijou deli,
O'Connell's pharmacy and the AIB.

The terrace just beside the Allied Irish Bank is **Victoria Terrace**, which was built in 1852.

Number 15 Victoria Terrace was home to two great local historians, Fred and Beatrice Dixon. Fred was English, and came to Ireland in 1936 to work in the Meteorological Service. He married Beatrice Butler in 1950, and they moved to Rathgar in 1953. They both had a lifelong interest in history, and indeed it continued in Beatrice's family. Beatrice's sister was Sister Kathleen Butler. All three were members of the Old Dublin Society (ODS), and read several papers there. Fred was an inveterate collector, and after his death in 1988, Beatrice bequeathed his collection to the Gilbert Library in Pearse Street. I have drawn on his vast collection for this book.

He viewed all history as an inheritance – to have, to use, but most essentially to pass on. The papers he read to the ODS ranged from the weather in old Dublin to Bianconi and Irish postal history. He became President of the society. I don't know how he would manage now, because he always had a pipe in his mouth. His knowledge was extensive, and he was generous in sharing it.

Number 33, Hopeton, was the home of Robert Browne, son of the founder of Brown Thomas. A window is dedicated to him in Zion church.

Number 33, Hopeton, the home of Robert Browne.

Another occupant was Supreme Court Judge James Creed Meredith (1875–1942). He was appointed to the Supreme Court in 1937.

Creed Meredith gained degrees from both the Royal University of Dublin (now UCD) and Trinity College, Dublin. He was called to the bar in 1901. His father, Sir James, was Secretary of the Royal University (1880–1909). The Royal ceased to exist and became University College, Dublin, when the National University of Ireland was established.

Creed Meredith was an outstanding student, both as an academic and as an athlete: he was the Irish 440 yards champion for four years, and won the English championship in 1896. He founded the Young Ireland branch of the United Irish League with Francis Cruise O'Brien (father of Conor Cruise O'Brien), Owen Sheehy Skeffington, Rory O'Connor, Tom Kettle and A.E. Malone – a veritable who's who of early twentieth-century historic figures.

In 1913, John Redmond nominated Creed Meredith to the Committee of the Irish Volunteers. He was an active member, unlike other nominees. When the arms shipment on board the *Asgard* was planned, he crewed on board Sir Thomas Myles's boat, the *Chotah*. They met the *Asgard* in the Irish Sea, took some of the arms from it and landed them in Kilcoole on 1 August 1913, the Howth landing having taken place the previous Sunday, 26 July.

During the War of Independence, the Provisional Government set up courts, and Creed Meredith was President of these courts. After Independence, he was appointed a High Court judge. He also served on several constitutional committees in the setting up of the State. One of his major influences was in the adoption of proportional representation as our voting system.

Creed Meredith married a French Canadian artist, Lorraine Seymour Percy. They had two daughters, Moira and Brenda. Moira's son is the renowned sculptor Rowan Gillespie. Creed Meredith was an avid art collector. He donated 'Low Tide' by Jack B. Yeats, and 'Girl in White' by Grace Henry, to the Dublin Municipal Gallery. He translated the work of the German philosopher Immanuel Kant. He remained friendly with the renowned Jesuit theologian Thomas Finlay all his life. He later joined the Religious Society of Friends, and is buried in their cemetery at Temple Hill, Blackrock.

One of the more dramatic events to occur in Rathgar was just before 3pm on Monday, 10 September 1934. A Fairey 3F aeroplane, piloted by local resident Arthur Russell and carrying two passengers, Sergeant Toomey and Sergeant Canavan, collided with trees and landed in the garden of 33 Terenure Road East, the residence of Supreme Court Justice Meredith. Arthur Russell and Sergeant Toomey were killed instantly. Sergeant Leo Canavan survived, but with serious burns.

The *Irish Times* report gives a bit more information:

Lt. Arthur Russell, one of the Free State Air Corps best airmen was testing a new Fairey machine over the outskirts of the city [Dublin] *when at a height of 500 ft, the machine went into a spin. The pilot righted it at 200 ft but it went into another spin and the machine crashed into the garden of Mr. Justice Meredith.*

Months later, the Court of Inquiry stated that 'it was flying at an unsafe altitude over a thickly populated area. It stalled and crashed after hitting a tree ending up between 31/33 Terenure Road East.'

The folklore of Rathgar relates two stories: one is that the pilot was throwing sweets to the children on his road; while the other story maintains that Arthur was showing off to his brother, who was watching from his front door. Maybe both are true.

Michael Dixon, on the Royal Air Force website rafcommands.com, states that in the 1970s, he spoke to Sergeant Leo Canavan, the sole survivor of the crash. Leo said that the officer was flying low to impress family and neighbours, when it struck trees. But Leo's abiding memory was the smell of burning flesh when the plane burst into flames after the crash.

You can imagine the reaction to the crash. Arthur's brother, Charles, was second in Command in Ireland's new Air Corps, and it was the only Fairey 3F aeroplane the Irish Airforce had in their possession!

In 1930, Charles and Arthur Russell were also honorary instructors of the Irish Aeroclub, based in Baldonnel. Another member of that club was Oliver St John Gogarty, who wrote, on hearing of Russell's death:

Of my friend Arthur Russell soldier and airman

He had the kind and languorous air

Of gentle knights detached from fear;

And he was quiet in his ways,

He could the heavens ablaze

And overtake the sinking sun

With speed and soar into his throne.

If modesty clothes bravery

If gentleness activity;

If earth has ever been the pen

Of heaven-aspiring denizen,

Then Arthur comes into his own,

From lowly things released and flown,

And stands for that haut chivalry

Which scorns the world and scales the sky;

So Death, which no brave spirit harms,

Let him pass out retaining arms.

Colonel Charles Russell lived close by, in **number 46**, named Claredon. Russell had enlisted in the RAF during the First World War. After the war, he went to Canada for a time, and then settled in London.

When the Irish War of Independence came to an end, the Treaty negotiations took place in London in the autumn of 1921. Among the delegates from Ireland was Michael Collins. At the time, he had a price of £10,000 on his head for his capture. His friend Emmet Dalton feared that if the negotiations broke down, Collins would be arrested by the British authorities. Russell was tasked with buying a Martinsyde Type A Mark 2 aircraft in order to fly Collins out of London quickly in that event. Dalton had the plane on standby nearby, and planned to transport Collins, along with three aides, to Bristol. From there, they would fly across to Rosslare, and then follow the rail tracks to land the plane at Leopardstown racecourse. The plane was christened *The Big Fellow*, which was Collins's nickname.

After the successful Treaty negotiations, the plane arrived at Baldonnel in June 1922. By October 1922, the plane had been repainted in the national colours, and the name *The Big Fella* was painted on its nose. In 1932, with the change of government, its name was changed to *City of Dublin*. Alas, the plane was scrapped in 1935.

In the 1950s, an Air Force officer submitted a script, due to be broadcast, about the aeroplane, for the approval of the Department of Defense. A request was made by the Department to change the name of the plane to *The Long Fella*, Éamon de Valera's nickname. The request was refused, and the script was broadcast in full with the original name. Sadly, all that is left of the plane is the propeller, which is in the Officers' Mess at Casement Aerodrome, Baldonnel.

HIGHFIELD ROAD

The left-hand side of Highfield Road, coming from the Rathmines direction, was the first to be developed. The right-hand side wasn't built on until the early 1900s. From the 1860s on, the lands on the right side were owned by Thomas Edward Villiers Tuthill, who lived in Rathgar Mansion, on Upper Rathmines Road. Villiers Tuthill's son Neville developed the lands, hence the names Neville and Villiers on the roads.

Highfield Road was the original road from Rathmines to Rathgar. Formerly known as Cross Avenue, it became Highfield Road in the mid-eighteenth century. The numbering system on Highfield Road starts at the Rathmines end.

Number 17 was the residence of Robert Cochrane (1846–1916), engineer, architect and antiquarian. He was an inspector for ancient monuments of Ireland and a surveyor with the Board of Works. Cochrane was editor of the *Journal of the Royal Society of Antiquaries of Ireland*, along with other publications.

Number 37 was the home of Patrick Sarsfield Ó hÉigeartaigh or, as he preferred to be known, Pádraig Sáirséal Ó hÉigeartaigh (1879–1955). He was secretary of the Post Office in 1922, and an avid book collector. His son was Seán Sáirséal Ó hÉigeartaigh, a teacher and staunch republican. It was because of his republicanism that he lost several teaching jobs. With his wife Brighid,

Looking up Highfield Road towards Rathgar village. Christ Church is on the left, and on the right is the entrance to Fairfield Park.

he founded the publishing company (1947–72) with a loan of £300 from Seán's aunt Eilís Dill Nic Gaghann. The title of the company was a combination of the two names.

The first book published by Sáirséal agus Dill was *Tonn Tuile* (1947) by Séamus Ó Néill. It sold 1,000 copies at 7/6d each. Among other authors the company published were Áine Yeats, Seán Ó Suilleabháin, Micheál Mac Liammóir, Máirtín Ó Cadhain, Máire Mhac an tSaoi, Pádraig Ó Laoi and Pádraic Ó Conaire.

Brighid would have been known around Rathgar, particularly because of her huge St Bernard dogs, whom she constantly spoke to in Irish. The book-selling tradition is being carried on by their son Cian, who for many years was a journalist in RTÉ.

Number 22 housed Miss Carr's preparatory school from the late 1940s to the 1970s. This was a feeder school for the private secondary schools of south Dublin.

Number 68 was the home of Erskine Childers (1905–74), President of Ireland from 1973 to 1974.

Erskine Hamilton Childers, son of Robert Erskine Childers and Mary Ellen Osgood, was born in London and educated at Trinity College, Cambridge. He spent holidays with his relatives in County Wicklow, and later returned to live in Ireland, becoming advertising manager of the newly founded *Irish Press*.

He entered politics and was elected as a Fianna Fáil deputy for the Athlone/Longford constituency in 1938. Having served in several ministries in Fianna Fáil governments, his last ministry being Health, he was elected President of Ireland in 1973. Sadly, a year later, having delivered a speech at the College of Physicians, he suffered a heart attack and died. He is buried in Roundwood, County Wicklow.

YORK ROAD

This is named after Philip Yorke, 3rd Earl of Hardwicke (1757–1834). He was Lord Lieutenant of Ireland from 1801 to 1806).

GARVILLE AVENUE

This is one of the oldest roads in Rathgar, first built on in the 1830s. The residents of this road would never characterise it as a hotbed of sedition and law-breaking, but, as the residents of numbers 14, 15 and 16 show, this was the case from 1911 to 1920.

Number 7 Upper Garville Avenue was the residence of Patrick Weston Joyce (1827–1914). Originally from County Limerick, he was one of fifteen teachers selected to reorganise the National School system in Ireland. His major work was his three-volume *The Origin and History of Irish Names of Places* (published in 1869, 1875 and 1913). He also wrote *A Social History of Ancient Ireland* (1903) and *English As We Speak It in Ireland* (1910). He was a noted collector of Irish music.

Number 14 was the home of Maurice MacGonigal PRHA (1900–79). Maurice was a cousin of Harry Clarke, and was apprenticed to Harry's father Joshua in his stained glass studios in North

Number 14 Garville Avenue, the home of republican and artist Maurice MacGonigal.

Frederick Street. In 1917, as a member of Na Fianna Éireann, he was interned in Kilmainham and later Ballykinlar camp. Although I couldn't find evidence for his involvement in blowing up Classon's Bridge beside the Dropping Well in 1920, the 3rd Battalion, of which he was a member, certainly was involved. He made many paintings of that particular area.

MacGonigal attended the Dublin Metropolitan School of Art. In 1924, he won the Taylor scholarship. He started teaching in the National College of Art in 1927, and became a member of the Royal Hibernian Academy in 1933. He was a prolific artist, especially of landscapes. He married Aida Sheppard, daughter of the sculptor Oliver Sheppard. He died in 1979, and his funeral was held in the Church of the Three Patrons, Rathgar. He was buried in Gurteen cemetery in Roundstone, Connemara, County Galway.

No 15 Garville Avenue. In 1912, Marjorie Haslor (died 1913) and Kathleen Houston lived here. They were members of the Irish Women's Franchise League, founded in Dublin in 1908 by Hanna Sheehy-Skeffington and Margaret Cousins.

To further the cause of women's suffrage, they embarked on a campaign of civil disobedience, arguing that they had been driven to law breaking, as constitutional means had been to no avail. They and their friends Hilda Webb and Maud Lloyd broke windows in several institutions in Dublin, among which was the GPO. They each received a six-month prison sentence. The Irish Women's Franchise League was the more militant wing of the Irish women's suffrage movement.

Jack Lynch, sporting hero and Taoiseach, who lived at number 21 Garville Avenue.

When sentenced, many of the women followed the English example of demanding political status, and went on hunger strike to obtain this status. This was the first hunger strike in modern Ireland. It commenced on 14 August 1912, according to Hanna Sheehy-Skeffington in *Reminiscences of an Irish Suffragette.*

Number 16 was the home of Kathleen Emerson. She was a member of the Irish Women's Suffragette Society, formed in 1872, and also a member of the Irish Women's Franchise League. She broke windows in the Custom House, and was also sentenced to six months in prison.

Number 16 was also home to Dr Conn Murphy, the first Doctor of Philosophy from the Royal University of Ireland. A founder of the Gaelic League and a staunch republican, his family were all involved in the struggle. During the War of Independence, the house was often raided.

Number 21 was the residence of Jack Lynch (1917–99). Jack was born in Cork. After leaving school he became a law clerk, and then studied law in University College, Cork, at night, completing his law degree at King's Inns in Dublin. Called to the bar in 1945, he returned to Cork.

During this period, he was renowned as an outstanding sportsman. He was the only man in GAA history to captain his county in both hurling and football in the same year, 1939. He won five All-Ireland hurling medals and one All-Ireland football medal.

He was first elected to Dáil Éireann for Fianna Fáil in 1948. He became a minister in 1955, and continued to serve in Cabinet in different posts until he succeeded Seán Lemass as Taoiseach in 1966. He was Taoiseach for two periods, 1966–73 and 1977–79. During his first term as Taoiseach, he presided over the referendum to ratify our entry into the European Economic Community (EEC), now the EU.

He had a turbulent period when two of his ministers were accused of giving money to the IRA to purchase arms. The money had been given by the Government for relief for victims of the crises in the North. The ministers he sacked were Charles Haughey and Neil Blaney, and Kevin Boland resigned in protest.

Lynch led Fianna Fáil to an overall majority in 1977's general election, the last time there was an overall majority in Ireland. The major policy they stood on was a plan to abolish rates. With divisions increasing in his party, Lynch resigned as Taoiseach in 1979, and retired from politics in 1981. Widely regarded as one of the most popular politicians in Ireland of the twentieth century, his last few years were dogged by ill-health. He died in 1999. He had a state funeral in the Church of the Sacred Heart, Donnybrook, and was buried in St Finbar's cemetery in his beloved Cork city.

Number 42 was the home of Constantine P. Curran (1883-1972), one of James Joyce's great friends. They met at the Royal University and remained lifetime friends. Curran took the iconic photo of James Joyce with his hands in his pockets. What Joyce was later asked what he was thinking about, he said, 'I was wondering if he would lend me five shillings.'

Among Curran's works are *Dublin Decorative Plasterwork*, *The Rotunda Hospital* and *James Joyce Remembered*.

GROSVENOR ROAD

On this site and beyond, the Grimwoods had their nursery. They also ran a seed shop at 1 Charlotte Street (now demolished), near Kelly's Corner. The nursery comprised about thirteen acres before Grosvenor and Kenilworth were laid out in 1860.

Grosvenor was named to evoke the exclusivity of the London address. The name derives from the French *gros veneur*, literally meaning 'great hunter'. It is the family name of the dukes of Westminster.

James Joyce as photographed by Constantine P. Curran in the back garden of his father's house, 6 Cumberland Place, North Circular Road.

The building of Grosvenor Road began around the late 1840s. One of the chief architects, who designed several houses, was E.H. Carson (1821–81), whose practice was at 25 South Frederick Street. A staunch Presbyterian, he had a practical side as well as an aesthetic one. His wife, Isabella Lambert, was related to a member of the Rathmines and Rathgar Township. Isabella had strong Protestant Orange leanings. She had an enormous influence on their son Edward Junior (1854–1935), who became a lawyer and Ulster politician, and founder of the Ulster Volunteers.

Edward Senior was a founder member of the Pembroke Township in 1861. His company developed much of Sallymount Avenue and Appian Way in Ranelagh. His family lived at 4 Harcourt Street, and then Sarzey, Rathgar Road.

In 1859, Edward Carson designed two houses on Frankfort Avenue, and four houses, numbers 53 to 56, on Grosvenor Road. In 1864, he designed Wakefield House, 7 Grosvenor Road. In 1878, he designed three houses on Winton Avenue.

Number 30 was the home of Fenian leader and journalist John O'Leary (1830–1907). He edited *The Irish People* with Tom Clarke and Charles Kickham. In 1896, he published *Recollections of Fenians and Fenianism*. He was arrested in 1865, convicted of 'treason felony' and sentenced to twenty years' penal servitude. This was reduced to exile in 1871, after which he mainly lived in Paris, but travelled to the US. In 1885, he returned to Ireland, and was highly regarded as a wise old republican in the cultural world of Dublin. He was remembered, of course, by W.B. Yeats in his poem 'September 1913':

Romantic Ireland's dead and gone,
It's with O'Leary in the grave.

In the poem, Yeats laments the fact that true romantic, idealistic men were no longer to be found in Ireland. John O'Leary died in 1907, and is buried in Glasnevin Cemetery.

Numbers 53 to 56 were, according to Jeremy Williams in *Architecture in Ireland*, 'the most ambitious "Gothic revival" speculative terrace built in the Dublin suburbs'. But even at number 1, you can see Gothic 'cut-outs' in the wall. So it appears to have been a popular style at the time. Several examples of the Gothic revival influence can be seen on the road.

Number 1 is St Louis's Convent. This was built in 1913, for the St Louis nuns. The order, founded in 1842, was approved by Rome in 1844. It was originally an order both for nuns and priests. The priestly part of the order lasted only six years, though the nuns continue on to the present day. Their first house in Ireland was in Carrickmacross, County Monaghan. The nuns here arrived from France, and they taught through the medium of French for the first thirty years or so. They opened their school in Rathmines on 1 September 1913, in Charleville, the former home of Sir John Gray.

Number 52, formerly the Jewish Congregation Hall, is now the Rathgar Parish Centre.

Numbers 62 and 63 house Rathgar Junior School, founded by Isabella Douglas, a Quaker, in 1919 (see Churchtown), and still thriving today. Miss Douglas was Fröebel trained, and was a strong advocate of the teaching of Irish.

Molesworth House was the residence of Reverend Christopher Teeling McCready (1837–1913), who was Curate Assistant in St Audoen's and Minor Canon of St Patrick's Cathedral. He is best remembered as author of *Dublin Street Names* (1892).

KENILWORTH SQUARE (1860)

Sir Walter Scott wrote a novel called *Kenilworth* (1821), from which Kenilworth derives its name. The Square was previously part of the Grimwood nurseries. It is not a square, but a parallelogram, with east and west equal in length but north longer than south.

The area began to be developed in the late 1850s, but the major development took place in the 1860s, with a few developers involved on different sites. These houses were large, built for a wealthy class. The dominant feature is the square itself. As with a lot of the earlier squares, such as Fitzwilliam or Merrion, the residents had the exclusive use of the square. In 1947, Mr White, a resident, purchased the lease for the square, with a view to building on it. He was refused planning permission. The Holy Ghost Fathers from St Mary's College, Rathmines, then purchased it as playing fields for the school, as all they had in Rathmines was the front pitch. Generations of international rugby stars trained and played here.

Number 31 Kenilworth Square, home of the Elvery
family of the Elvery Sports shops.

The number 18 tram, known as the tram 'to the sea', ran from Kenilworth Square to Sandy-mount. When the tram ceased, the bus took the number of the route.

Number 3, Kenilworth House, is an interesting one, built in the Greek revivalist fashion.

Number 18 was home to the Pile family. Sir Thomas was Lord Mayor in 1902, and his family ran the Kenilworth Hotel here.

Number 30 was where Charles Eason (1823–99) of Eason's bookshop fame lived. He had previously been a manager in W.H. Smith in Belfast, and when he opened his shop in Dublin, there was an agreement that W.H. Smith would not open in competition. He had previously lived in Brighton Avenue.

Number 31 was the home of John West Elvery. His father William Elvery came from Sussex and, with a great interest in leisure and sports, founded the Elvery Sports shop in Wicklow Street. Later the company moved to Suffolk Street. His daughter was the artist Beatrice Elvery, later Lady Glenavy. She published her autobiography with the intriguing title *Today We Will Only Gossip* (1964).

Number 32 was the home of Dr White, Professor of Divinity and Canon of St Patrick's Cathedral.

Number 39 was where Thomas Holmes Mason (1877–1958) lived. Mason ran a family business at 5/6 Dame Street, as opticians, photographic dealers and laboratory furnishers. He was the fifth generation of Masons to do so. His hobbies are of more interest: Meteorology was a major one, and from this house, measurements of rainfall, sunshine, wind speed and temperature were supplied to the newspapers every day. He had a reputation as a very accurate long-range weather forecaster.

Mason was also a keen photographer, and amassed over 20,000 photos. He was a keen archaeologist and zoologist. He was a member and President of Dublin Zoo, and President of An Taisce. He published a book entitled *The Islands of Ireland: Their scenery, people, life and antiquities* (1950). In 1931, he was elected to the Royal Irish Academy. Mason died in 1958, and is buried in Mount Jerome Cemetery, Harold's Cross. The company, Mason Technology, continues still.

Number 44 Dudley Lodge, next to Murphy & Gunn, is considered to be the oldest house in Kenilworth. It dates from the early 1840s.

Number 50 was home to Ernest Blythe (1889–1975), who was born into a Presbyterian family in County Antrim. He came to Dublin aged fifteen, and became a fluent Irish speaker. Upon an invitation from Seán O'Casey, he joined the IRB, and he was elected as TD for Monaghan in 1918. He was Saorstát Éireann's first Minister of Finance and, as such, was always remembered as the man who took a shilling off the old age pensioners, reducing their pension from ten to nine shillings. As a result of this action, he was subsequently defeated in the 1932 election.

In 1936, Blythe resigned from politics and devoted himself to the theatre. He was Managing Director of the Abbey theatre from 1941 to 1967. This was another career that did not win him approval from all quarters, because it was felt that he had his own idiosyncratic way of selecting plays to be performed. He is buried in Glasnevin Cemetery.

Number 51 was the home of Sybil and Albert Le Brocquy, after their first house on Zion Road. The Rutland Memorial Fountain in Merrion Square is dedicated to Sybil Le Brocquy (1892–1973), 'whose enthusiasm for life, literature, and the Arts enriched many lives'. It was unveiled by President Cearbhall Ó Dálaigh on 16 June 1976.

Above: Revolutionary, Taoiseach and President Eamon de Valera.

Below: A newspaper ad for William Sheppard's landscaping services.

Number 53 was used by Éamon de Valera as a headquarters when another house in Blackrock was raided in 1921. He met here with Arthur Griffith when Griffith returned from the Treaty negotiations in London, to try to resolve their differences. Sadly, it didn't work.

Number 74 was the home of landscape gardener William Sheppard (1842–1923). He ran his business at 20 Oxford Road, Rathmines.

It was thought that Rathgar residents always had a genteel air about them. This is best summed up in Jimmy O'Dea and Fred O'Donovan's words:

Thank heavens, we are living in Rathgar

In these days of agitators,

Isms, schisms and dictators,

When one never knows whom one is talking to;

When we've princes picking winners

And we've plumbers at golf dinners,

It's so difficult to really say who's who.

Even at our rugby dances

One's beset by vulgar glances,

And our finer sensibilities are shocked.

'pon my soul I'm not romancing,

We are more danced against than dancing,

And the flappers come and tell you they're half cocked.

So, thank heavens, we are living in Rathgar.

O the solid, quiet refinement of Rathgar,

Where we have our evening dinners,

Where we never hear of Shinners,

And even those who can't afford it have a car.

There are some quite decent suburbs, I am sure.

O Rathmines is not so bad or Terenure.

O we've heard of spots like Inchicore,

But really don't know where they are;

For, thank heavens, we are living in Rathgar.

Someone must live in Kilmainham,

So it's hardly fair to blame 'em,

And in Dartry they are almost civilised.

But in Fairview, goodness gracious,

Fellows tennis in their braces;

In Drumcondra all their shirts are trubenised.

Although it's worth relating,

It's really devastating,

At Baldoyle I saw my butcher in the ring.

So what with cinemas unsightly,

And the Gaiety gone twice nightly,

It's no wonder that we're proudly forced to sing …

That, thank heavens, we are living in Rathgar.

O the solid, quiet refinement of Rathgar.

In Killester they eat cockles

And those fearful things – pigs' knuckles;

But you've never heard of tripe in Grosvenor Square.

O those accents on the Northside quite appal,

But they never get beyond Rathmines Town Hall.

They've so many kids in Kimmage

That they say life's just a scrimmage …

(Oh I'm tired – I'm going to the Buttery to have one …)

So, thank heavens, we are living in Rathgar.

LASWADE
CASANA

M OBRIEN©
2019

CHURCHTOWN

Churchtown Cemetery, Dundrum.

CHURCHTOWN

I t is called Churchtown, but where is the church? The area of Churchtown was established around the church of St Nahi. In fact, the townland areas of Churchtown Upper and Lower are to the east of Lower Churchtown Road. Churchtown as we know it today includes these, but also the townlands of Newtown Little, Rathmines Little and Great, and Whitehall. It is in the ancient parishes of Rathfarnham and Taney.

Taney gets its name from St Nahi, a follower of St Maulruain in Tallaght in the eighth century. Tallaght had a huge monastic settlement, but Nahi wanted to found his own settlement. The split is nothing new in Ireland. So Nahi came through the fields and forests, and picked an area on top of a hill in Dundrum, where St Nahi's church now stands, next to the Dargan (Luas) bridge. It was a good site for a monastic community – at the top of a hill, it had a good view, and there was a constant supply of water at the bottom of the hill from the River Slang, the river that runs through Dundrum Town Centre. Nahi lived where the little church is now. It was known as Teach Nahi, which became anglicised to Taney.

In 1192, Pope Celestine granted land to the Archbishop of Dublin at Taulaghe (Taney). In the Black Book (*Liber Niger*), the parish was listed in the diocese of Dublin, and Archbishop Luke gave the church of Taney the prebendary stall which was for the benefit of the parish. Taney is often referred to as being 'in the prebendal dignity of the Archdeacon of Dublin'. In 1326, the Archbishop had two cantreds here, a cantred being a measurement of land, a subdivision of a county. Hence the name Churchtown – land that belonged to the Church. Just a minor point: it was pronounced *Taw*-ney, not *Tay*-ney as now.

St Nahi's Church and graveyard, with Dargan Bridge in the background.

When John Le Bret, Sheriff of Dublin, inspected the lands in 1326, he noted of Newtown that five tenants held fifty-five acres: 'At Milltown and Thanoly are tenants English and Irish holding 4 score acres at 3d per year peace, nothing in war.'

William Petty in his survey of Ireland in 1654 says, 'the parish consists of 1,507 acres of which 88 belong to the Archbishop of Dublin'.

Oliver Cromwell was, of course, the first republican. After he assumed control of England, he decided to conquer Ireland, and he arrived in Ringsend on 15 August 1649. The Battle of Rathmines had just taken place on 2 August. Briefly, the battle was between the Marquis of Ormond – Lord Lieutenant of Ireland under the now deposed King Charles, representing the old order – and Colonel Michael Jones, the new Parliamentary Commander of Dublin.

In June 1649, Ormond advanced on Dublin, hoping to reclaim it from Jones. *Irish Battles* (1969) by G.A. Hayes-McCoy gives a full account of the battle, which ultimately ended in Ormond's defeat.

After Oliver Cromwell had subdued Ireland, like all conquerors, he wanted to exact money from the country. Cromwell also had to pay his troops, and he decided to give them land, Irish land, in lieu of money. In order to do this, the land had to be surveyed, and to this end he appointed William Petty (1623–87), who had come to Ireland with Cromwell as Physician-General. In addition to being a medical man, Petty was also one of the great economic philosophers. He advocated a laissez-faire economic attitude of government, and was among the first to theorise about division of labour – where specialists would work at one specific task on several projects, rather than everybody doing everything on one project.

Petty trained people to survey the land in what became known as the Down Survey. Chains with 100 links were used to measure the land. This was a unit of measurement – sixty-six feet or twenty-two yards in total. The chains had to be laid *down* on the ground, and hence the name 'Down', though some say it was because the results were written down.

Petty completed the survey in the years 1654–56, and it was published in 1685. He was well paid, receiving 30,000 acres around Kenmare, County Kerry, plus £9,000. Although a Cromwellian, he received royal approval afterwards, and was knighted in 1661. He was a founder member of the Royal Society of London. The methods he used were much like the census of today.

SANATIVE AIR

In the eighteenth and nineteenth centuries, Dundrum and Churchtown were well known for their restorative powers. Dublin city at this time was smog- and disease-ridden. It was felt that a week in the country could restore health to any ailing person, but needless to say, this option was only available to the wealthy.

Aside from the clear mountain air, there was fresh goats' milk available. When milk is left to curdle, it splits into solids and liquids. Whey is the watery liquid, and curds are the solid parts used to make cheese. Whey was considered then as a tonic, and today it is used by body-builders, recognised for its high protein content.

The visiting season to Dundrum and Churchtown was from April to May, and then again from September to October. The whey got too thick and wasn't very nice from June on, though you could chance diluting it in June and July, the proportion being one pint of water to four ounces of whey. Whey was never to be taken in August. Fashions are copied the world over, and in England in 1802, the rhyme 'Little Miss Muffett' showed the popularity of consuming whey.

Little Miss Muffett
Sat on her tuffet,
Eating her curds and whey …

An early Irish poem also promoted the benefits of goats' milk:

Is leigheas air gach tinn	Garlic with May butter
Cheamh'us is a mhaigh	Cureth all disease
Ol' an flochair sid	Drink of goat's white milk
Bainne ghobhar bán	Take along with these

A Taste of Ireland (1968) by Theodora Fitzgibbon

TRANSPORT

Churchtown was in the country, and the only way to travel, if you didn't own your own horse, was by jaunting car. J.N. Brewer, in his *Beauties of Ireland* (1826), describes how 'Numerous jaunting cars convey from the city large parties of visitors to partake of that sanative beverage … the reviving scenery over which the animals browsed.' Brewer believed in flowery language.

George Turbett ran a jaunting car service in 1803, from the city centre to Dundrum. The journey was priced at 1s.3d inside and 10d outside, for a single journey. There was no riffraff out here at those prices! Later, from the 1860s on, there were big houses in the area, and the owners had their own horses and carriages. The whole area seems to have been infected with foot and mouth disease in 1883, and this happened several times over the next hundred years.

WHITEHALL

As I have stated, Churchtown never had a village, and even now its centre is a supermarket and a green area, both privately owned. When the modern church was being built, it is a pity that it was not located where Camberley Oaks is now. This would have acted as a nucleus for the village to grow up around. As the church is located quite a distance from these shops, the area lacks a focus. In fact, the main focus is SuperValu. The original supermarket was established in the late 1950s by H. Williams and Company.

Churchtown Green, showing Churchtown Stores, Meadows & Byrne, Insomnia café, the post office, Howard's Way restaurant, Lloyds pharmacy and Jim Tracey's SuperValu supermarket.

The hardware shop used to be a grocer's, owned by John Connolly. The Churchtown Stores used to stay open 364 days a year. It stocked everything from A to Z, in a storage system that only the staff could begin to decipher. It is now the Churchtown Stores pub.

P.V. Doyle (1923–88) opened his first pub, the County Club, on the south side of the green in the 1950s. Doyle was one of the great developers of the 1950s and 1960s. He was also on the finance committee for Archbishop of Dublin Dr J.C. McQuaid. This certainly helped Doyle to establish contacts and, even more importantly, it gave him links to the planning department of Dublin County Council.

In several areas of Dublin, it can be seen that where the Archbishop got planning for a new church, Doyle got planning nearby for one of his many developments. The Doyle family went on to control a chain of hotels.

Churchtown was a developing area, and Doyle was in the vanguard of developers when he built the pub. The pub was sold to a Mr Shannon, who in 1959 sold it to Ned Finnegan for £16,000. As well as being a pub, the County Club had an upmarket restaurant, silver service and linen-covered tables being the order of the day. It was *the* place to go in the area.

Finnegan built the Bottle Tower pub in 1962, and it was run by the Finnegan family up until 2015. Even though it is located around the corner from the County Club, it is in the county rather than the city, as the county boundary runs between the two pubs. This was significant for men who did not want their drinking interrupted. City pubs had what was comically called a 'holy hour', between 2.30pm and 3.30pm, when the pubs would shut so that men would go home. The term 'holy hour' comes from a Catholic religious service, 'devotions', which used to last about an hour. But when holy hour rolled around, customers of the County Club would simply nip around the corner to the Bottle Tower.

Finnegan eventually sold the County Club, which became the Braemor Rooms, and quickly established itself as the major entertainment venue of south County Dublin. All the international stars and Irish showbands of the time performed there.

Next door to the Braemor Rooms was a bookmaker's shop, or a 'turf accountant' to give them their former name. This was situated where the Paddy Power sign is now. The shop was owned by P.J. Kilmartin; he and his brother T.A. had seventy bookmaker's shops all over the city.

They were the dingiest places you could imagine, where a crackly Tannoy system would just give you the results of the races. Horse racing was the only sport there was to bet on. If you were lucky, they would sellotape a sheet of paper with the results on to the window when the shop was closed. It was all a far cry from today, where one of the leading companies on the Irish stock exchange is a bookmaker!

THE DUBLIN AND SOUTH EASTERN RAILWAY

William Dargan, the man who developed the railways in Ireland, was born in Carlow in 1799. After leaving school, his first job was as an assistant to the famous engineer Thomas Telford, who constructed the road from Holyhead to Chester in Anglesea, Wales.

Having impressed his superiors, he then got the job of building the road from Howth Harbour, where the mail boat came in, to Dublin. Then, in 1834, the first railway line was built from Dublin to Kingstown, now Dún Laoghaire, and Dargan was involved in its construction. This was the world's first commuter railway line. Dargan then calculated, rightly, that railways were going to be the chosen mode of transport for getting around the country. He proceeded to build railways all over Ireland.

He and his co-directors built a railway line out to Dundrum. Originally called the Dublin and Wicklow Railway, it became the Dublin and South Eastern Railway (DSER), running from Harcourt Street to Bray, County Wicklow. It opened on 10 July 1854. On this line, the building of the Nine Arches Bridge, spanning the Dodder at Milltown, represents one of the great engineering feats of Irish railway construction. The DSER railway was christened by the Dubs the Dublin Slow and Easy Railway, or Damn Seldom Ever Repaired, but also the Dublin Swift and Energetic Railway.

Dargan was no fool, and this was a money-making activity. Railway travel was expensive and exclusive – it was said you could travel on the train from Dundrum to Dublin without meeting a Catholic, save for the conductor. The big Luas bridge (2004) spanning Dundrum is deservedly named after William Dargan.

As William Dargan lived in Mount Anville, it was always felt that his local station, in Dundrum, was more sophisticated than other stations on the Harcourt Street line. In fairness,

The Nine Arches bridge at Milltown, as seen in an old postcard.

it was during construction that the decision was made to extend the line to Bray, and not to have the terminus in Dundrum as originally planned.

When Dargan bought Mount Anville in Goatstown, he commissioned John Skipton Mulvaney to redesign the house. Mulvaney also designed Broadstone railway station, the Royal Irish Yacht Club in Dún Laoghaire, and Longfield Terrace and Belgrave Square in Monkstown. England's Queen Victoria came to Ireland in 1853 and called to Mount Anville to visit Dargan. She offered him a knighthood, but he refused. While she was in Mount Anville, she planted a Wellingtonian pine tree, which still grows today. The *Dublin Evening Post* of 31 August 1853 states:

Her Majesty at a quarter to 5 o'clock, in a chariot drawn by four splendid bays and attended by five outriders, drove out of the gates of the Vice Regal Lodge in Phoenix Park. There was a second chariot with other members of the Royal Party and all arrived at "Mount Anville" at 5.30 pm. The Royal party which included Prince Albert and the Prince of Wales [later Edward VII] *were received by Mr. and Mrs. Dargan.*

They were conducted through the splendid mansion to the adjoining lofty tower from which they obtained a view not to be surpassed for grandeur, beauty and variety in the United Kingdom. Her Majesty and His Royal Highness expressed their warmest admiration for the scenery. After paying a visit of more than an hour's duration, they returned to the Phoenix Park where they arrived at 7 o'clock passing through Kilmainham on the way.

William Dargan sold Mount Anville to the Sisters of the Sacred Heart in 1865, and they founded a school there that still flourishes today.

Dargan also set up the National Gallery in Merrion Square, after he had inspired and financed the Great Exhibition of 1853. His statue stands outside the Gallery, sculpted by Sir Thomas Farrell (1827–1900), who also created Lord Ardilaun's statue in St Stephen's Green.

William Dargan died in 1867, eventually succumbing to injuries sustained by falling from a horse. He spent the last two years of his life at 2 Fitzwilliam Square, Dublin. Perhaps it is best to leave the last word to Gothic author Sheridan Le Fanu: 'I have never met a man more quick in intelligence, more clear-sighted and more thoroughly honourable.' What a marvellous epitaph to have!

The Harcourt Street Line was closed down on 31 December 1958. It was always said that it was closed by Todd Andrews, Chairman of Córas Iompair Éireann (CIÉ), but in all fairness to him, he was implementing government policy under Taoiseach Éamon de Valera. Thankfully we now have as a replacement, the Luas Green Line, launched on 30 June 2004. The name Luas is the Irish word for speed.

In the years following the Second World War, when development was beginning in the area, the number 61 bus, a single-decker, ran from Burgh Quay to Churchtown via Ranelagh and Milltown. The terminus was at Hillside Drive. Another bus, number 47A, also a single-decker, came to Churchtown via Rathmines and Rathgar, then up Orwell Road as far as Green Park, beside Milltown golf course. This changed to a double-decker, and the route was extended to terminate also at Hillside Drive. The numbers 47A and 61, because of the location of their termini, were regarded as 'polite' buses, as the people who travelled on them were considered to have 'an air' about them. These routes were thought by the conductors and drivers to be easy routes. The 47A route was discontinued, and the 61 still goes to Churchtown but via a very circuitous route, from D'Olier Street to Whitechurch, Rathfarnham.

The number 14 ran through Rathmines and Milltown, and had its terminus on Braemor Road. Latterly, the number 14A route was established and its terminus was on Beaumont Avenue, Churchtown. Now the number 14 runs from the northside suburb of Beaumont, through the city, through Rathgar village, on to Orwell Road Braemor Road and Ballinteer, and down to the Dundrum Luas station. The 14A is discontinued.

Numbers 16 and 16A came to Churchtown from town via Rathfarnham, terminating at Nutgrove Avenue. The 16 now runs from Dublin Airport to Ballinteer. The 16A is discontinued.

In 1825, the first public railway to be built was the Stockton and Darlington Railway, which operated in northeast England. Built by Quaker businessman Edward Pease, it became known as the 'Quaker line'.

The Dublin and Wicklow railway line, later named the Dublin and South Eastern Railway (DSER), was opened in 1854. The Board of the Dublin and Wicklow line was composed of some Quaker businessmen and William Dargan. Quakers were to have a major influence on Churchtown.

The 47A bus makes its way down Orwell Road.

Right: Guinness stout, bottled by the Dropping Well pub.
Bottom: Churchtown Quaker Meeting House.

CHURCHTOWN/QUAKERSTOWN

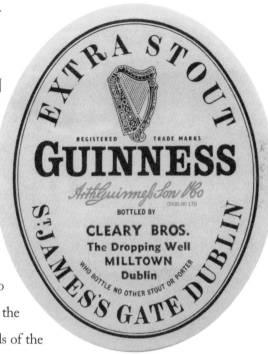

This heading may seem odd, but the late Eileen Veale told me that when she moved into Lower Churchtown Road in the 1930s, the area was colloquially known as Quakerstown.

During the 1850s and 1860s, a great evangelical zeal swept through England and Ireland. South County Dublin was no exception. At this time in Rathgar, just on the other side of the River Dodder, churches were being built to cater for the needs of the

M. O'Brien 4/19©

growing population. The Presbyterians built Christ Church (1862), while a proprietary church was built on Zion Road (1861), and later a parish church. Roman Catholics opened the Three Patrons Church in 1862, while the Baptists erected Grosvenor Road Church in 1859.

If you come up Lower Churchtown Road from the Dropping Well pub, before you approach the first set of traffic lights you will see, on your left, an entrance with granite piers. In faded letters on the left pier is written FRIENDS MEETING HOUSE. This meeting house has been here for 150 years.

The Religious Society of Friends, or Quakers, was founded by George Fox in England in 1652. William Edmundson, a follower of Fox's and formerly one of Cromwell's soldiers, came to Lurgan in 1654, where he set up his first meeting house. In 1655, Dublin held its first meeting, in the house of Richard Foukes, a tailor, at Polegate, near present-day Werburgh Street. From here, the Quakers spread south to Kilkenny, Waterford, Cork and other counties.

The followers were constantly harassed by the authorities; they were treated with the same prejudice as Catholics and Dissenters. William Penn, who had converted to the Religious Society of Friends while a student at Oxford, and expelled from there for his pains, came to Ireland in 1667, to manage his father's estates in East Cork, near Macroom. He came to Dublin in 1669, and met with the Lord Lieutenant to present a petition outlining the sufferings of fellow members. Penn went on to America, where he founded the Commonwealth in Delaware, and the State of Pennsylvania is named in his honour. Quakerism was the largest growing religion in North America in the seventeenth century.

Quakers follow the doctrine of inner truth, 'To thine own self be true.' They have no priests or ministers, and no oaths. Founded as they were out of conflict, their Peace Testimony is a central tenet of their faith. They also argued for the non-payment of tithes. Tithes were one tenth part of a worker's income, paid to the Government to fund the established Church, i.e. the Church of England. At their foundation, the Friends dressed and lived simply. The Friends' code was strict. If a member committed an offence in public, he or she was asked to apologise in public at the next meeting. If a Friend married outside the membership, he or she and their family were 'disowned', i.e. barred from the meeting. This policy led to talk that all Quakers were mad, due to intermarrying.

A strong ethos of mutual support grew up among the members. If a Friend got into financial difficulties, he would be helped, but if he ignored the advice of the meeting, he and his family could be disowned.

The Quakers became renowned for their honesty in business and commercial dealings, with fair measure, reasonable prices and good quality being their dictum. This quotation from Richard Allen, who ran a tailoring shop in Sackville Street, exemplifies their ethos:

I respect fully to my mode of conducting business. My rule is to purchase for cash from the manufacturing houses, I spare no pains in procuring the best foremen and workmen and by selling at a modest profit I offer purchasers every advantage the fair trader can extend.

In fact, it is said that Allen was responsible for the break-up of the monopolies of the Trade Guilds in Dublin. It was he that challenged the protectionist policies of the Tailors' Guild. Of course, the Guilds were the preserve of the established Church, and in the early eighteenth century, they ruled the city. Allen was also heavily involved in the anti-slavery and peace movements.

Joseph Rowntree, of confectionary fame, chaired a committee in the 1860s that led to the relaxation of the strict rules of the Society. He felt that if the status quo persisted, the Quakers would end up with no members at all.

Where the Quakers really wore their ethos on their sleeve was during the Irish 'famine' of 1847. At the very beginning of the famine in 1845, Quakers formed a Famine Relief Committee, with Joseph Bewley and Jonathan Pim both serving as secretaries. These were successful businessmen, with commercial contacts throughout the country, and through these connections, they set up a successful network throughout Ireland. They collected money, procured fifty large boilers from a Quaker family in Derby named Coalbrookdale (this firm also built the Wellington or Ha'penny Bridge over the Liffey in 1816), and set up soup kitchens all over the country. The Quakers were non-proselytising, and they worked to educate the impoverished people, as well as supplying seeds, agricultural equipment and fishing tackle.

The toll on the two businessmen was considerable, and Joseph Bewley died in 1851, many saying it was due to exhaustion. Jonathan Pim finally wound up the Committee, saying that the only solution to the problem of starvation was land reform.

In the 1850s, a lot of Quakers set up businesses in England: Wedgewood in pottery, Clark in shoes, Cadbury and Rowntree in confectionary. The Lloyd and Barclay families went into banking.

CHURCHTOWN LODGE

Among the Quakers in Churchtown was a businessman called Charles Malone. Charles's father had set up a business around 1800. In 1859, Malone was trading as Malone & Co at 41 George's Street. The business sold the 'finest Assam tea' at five shillings per pound. In the 1850s, Malone lived in Churchtown Lodge, while his brother Isaac lived across the road in Churchtown Park. Their father lived in Sweet Mount House, so they would have been familiar with the area. In all they owned about 100 acres.

Many Quakers had been involved in building the railway that opened in the 1850s. Charles, on hearing that a railway line was going to be built from Dundrum to Rathfarnham and also from Dundrum to Rathmines, decided to buy all the land on what is now both sides of Lower Churchtown Road, to sell on at a profit.

According to minute books of the Society of the time, many members had been holding meetings in houses in the area, rather than travelling to Rathmines or to the main Meeting House in Eustace Street.

Malone donated three roods (three quarters of an acre) to the Society, and on this they built a new meeting house. As was common at the time, the lease stated:

All mines, minerals, collieries, quarries and all other royalties and all wood and timber trees with ingress and regress to search for and carry away the same and liberty to hunt hawk fish and fowl on said plot.

The deed was witnessed by John Mullen of Weston House, Churchtown, and Alfred Hancock from Middleton, County Cork, both of whom swore the oath (they were clearly not Quakers, as Quakers do not take oaths). It was signed on 1 November 1861, and a yearly rent of one penny was payable if demanded.

Churchtown Meeting House was built at a cost of £820, with subscriptions of £641 and 15 shillings. It was opened in the tenth month, as the Quakers referred to October – months were referred to numerically back then, as Quakers objected to the use of pagan gods' names.

Unfortunately for Malone, the proposed railway did not materialise, and he went bankrupt in 1868. At that stage, Churchtown Meeting House was already in use. However, he got back on his feet quickly, and in 1869 had a business just down from the Four Courts at 12 Ormond Quay, where he sold 'The Judges Tea' at 2/6 per pound – half the price he was charging for his tea in George's Street. Malone later opened another two shops – one at 170 Great Brunswick Street, and the other at 29 North Earl Street. He lived in Clarendon House on Terenure Road East until he died. There seems to be no evidence of his attending any Friends' meeting house. He is buried in Mount Jerome Cemetery, which would indicate that he was not a member when he died.

WOODLAWN HOUSE

The treasurer of the Meeting House was a man called Adam Woods, who lived in Woodlawn House. Though Woodlawn House still exists, it is overshadowed by the Dargan (Luas) Bridge in Dundrum. Woods was a very wealthy businessman, trading at 20 Temple Lane and 8 Crow Street. A member of the Grand Jury of County Dublin, and Chairman of the local Dundrum Gas Board, Woods was also a very strong believer in temperance.

Adam Woods (left), temperance activist.

The original temperance movement was founded in Cork by a Quaker called William Martin, who used to take a glass of punch as a nightcap. To further the cause of moderate drinking, Martin enlisted the help of Father Theobald Mathew. Much against his family's wishes, Martin decided to abstain fully, as Father Mathew felt the only way forward was total abstinence. Perhaps the statues in O'Connell Street, Dublin, and in Cork City should be of Martin and not of Theobald Mathew.

Father Mathew (1790–1856) is often thought of as a Corkman, but he was in fact born in Thomastown, Golden, County Tipperary. He entered Maynooth to become a priest, but was expelled from there. He joined the Capuchin Order in Cork, and was ordained a Capuchin priest. He was extraordinarily successful at persuading the populace to abstain from alcohol. In 1838, the first year of the Temperance Movement, he enlisted nearly 200,000 people to take 'the pledge', as abstaining was called. It had a dramatic effect on the social order of Ireland. He died on 8 December 1856 in Cobh, and is buried in St Joseph's Cemetery, Cork.

Adam Woods was a member of the National Association for the Promotion of Social Science, and also of the United Kingdom Alliance for the Suppression of Traffic of Intoxicating Liquors. In 1872, he sat on a committee campaigning for the closure of public houses on Sundays. Woods, among the most influential people in the city, headed a deputation to the Lord Lieutenant. He also went to Arthur Guinness (later Lord Ardilaun), to enlist his support. Guinness was in something of a bind, as he mixed in this social circle, but he also knew where his income came from.

A plebiscite was ordered, the result of which was 28,181 votes in favour of closing on Sundays, to 3,104 votes against it. In this, Woods was supported by a number of Presbyterians and Catholics. In fact, the Diocese of Ferns under the influence of a Dr Furlong, followed by the Diocese of Cashel under the influence of a Dr Leahy, ordered the public houses to close on Sundays.

The law requiring public houses to close on Sundays was enacted in a piecemeal way. But changes in opening and closing hours on Sunday were always hotly debated in Ireland, and still are. Up until the 1960s, pubs opened on Sundays from 12.30pm to 2.30pm and from 5.30pm to 7.30pm. From then on, pubs were allowed to remain open from 5.30pm to 10.00pm. More recently, opening hours have extended radically.

When Woods died in 1901, he owned all of the land which is now Woodlawn, Churchtown House and Churchtown Lodge, Sweet Mount, Briar House, Charleville, Granite House, Frankfurt House, Fern Bank and Woodville.

A poem written around this time called 'A sup of good whiskey' includes the verse:

The Quakers will bid from drink abstain
By yea, and by nay, 'tis a fault in the vain;
Yet some of the broadbrims will get to the stuff,
And tipple away till they've tippled enough;
For Stiff-rump and Steady,
And Solomon's Lady
Would all take a sup in their turn.

THORNCLIFFE HOUSE, ORWELL ROAD

John Wardell originally had his business in Harold's Cross. He then went into partnership with a fellow Quaker, William Baker. They formed the company Baker Wardell, which first traded at 47 Thomas Street, and then moved to 75/76 Thomas Street, on the corner of Francis Street. Baker Wardell were tea, coffee, sugar and spice merchants. The company still exists, now trading as Robert Roberts and still selling coffee, amongst other products. Wardell was a marvellous self-publicist. In those days there were numerous Charity Sermons and the subscribers to these were listed in the front page of the *Irish Times*. Wardell's name was to be found there regularly. This was a cheap way of advertising.

As the company grew, Wardell became a very wealthy man. He built Thorncliffe House on an estate of ten acres in the 1860s. He also collected art, and built a gallery onto his house to exhibit works. At his death, he had what was regarded as the biggest private art collection in Ireland. One of the paintings, 'The Hellfire Club' by James Worsdale, can be seen in the National Gallery, having been donated to the gallery in his will.

Wardell was involved in horse racing, and had a stud farm in Dunboyne. He won the Irish Derby in 1874 with Ben Battle (at 5/2), and in 1878 with Madame Dubarry (at 5/1). Madame Dubarry is one of only eight fillies to win the Irish Derby to date. Peter Pearson (author of *The Heart of Dublin*, 2001) tells how Wardell used to race horses under his wife's maiden

Thorncliffe House and environs, seen from the air.

name of Dennison, so as not to alert the Quaker elders to his racing activities, for fear of being 'disowned'. All went fine until one of his horses won a race and his photo appeared in the newspaper. Whether he was disowned or left the Society, history doesn't relate, but when he died in 1878, he was buried in Mount Jerome Cemetery, according to the Church of Ireland rite.

Later residents of Thorncliffe House included Christopher Pallas (1831–1920), who was Lord Chief Baron of the Exchequer. He rented Thorncliffe in 1885. Educated at Clongowes Wood and Trinity College, Dublin, he was called to the bar in 1853. He became Solicitor-General in 1872, advancing to Attorney-General later that same year. He was appointed Lord Chief Baron in 1874, a position he held until 1916. This was an impressive achievement, as he was a devout Catholic and, at the age of forty-two, the youngest judge since Tudor times. He was regarded as a most learned judge, and his legal determinations are still quoted. When he was eighty, he drew up the Constitution of the National University of Ireland. He left Thorncliffe House, and moved to Cedarmount, opposite Mount Anville House, where he died in 1920.

Thorncliffe House was then rented to a man the Baron would have known well – William Walsh, the Catholic Archbishop of Dublin. He came to Thorncliffe House 'to take the country air', from 1888 to 1890. He thought about founding his palace here, but eventually settled on Drumcondra Road. He was known as 'Billy the lip'.

This rhyme came originally from a poem by James Joyce, 'Gas from the Burner' (1912):

For everyone knows the Pope can't belch
Without the consent of Billy Walsh.

Two sisters named Egan lived in Thorncliffe House for the next ten years, and Fred Woods bought it in 1899. Woods, the son of Adam Woods of Woodlawn House, lived here until 1937. In 1939, the well-known furrier Taylor Vard owned it, and the last owner of Thorncliffe House was one Mr Moscow.

In the 1950s, well-known show-jumper Captain Ronnie MacMahon schooled his horses at Thorncliffe House. In 1959, when Milltown Golf Club was burnt, Thorncliffe House was used as a club house.

The first houses of Thorncliffe Park estate were built in the early 1930s, and building continued at intervals. Thorncliffe House was demolished in 1962, to make way for the last houses of the estate.

FERNDALE

Ferndale, on Upper Churchtown Road, was the home of John McDonnell Green, who traded at 8 Burgh Quay as Green Brothers and Dublin Granaries Co. Ltd. He planted Scots pine trees to celebrate the birth of each of his children, and these trees still stand in the grounds.

Arthur Jacob (1790–1874) was a resident of Ferndale, and was one of the best-known ocular pathologists of his time. Professor of Anatomy and Physiology at the Royal College of Surgeons from 1826, he is known to this day for a membrane in the eye called Jacob's membrane.

In 1952, Archbishop John Charles McQuaid invited the Congregation of Notre Dame des Missions (founded in Caen, France, in 1861) to open a school. The sisters bought Ferndale in the same year, and opened a secondary school in January 1953 with five pupils. They expanded in 1955, buying Woodville. Notre Dame School was officially opened by Archbishop McQuaid in October 1958, and a junior school was constructed and opened in 1975. The school closed in 2017.

LANDSCAPE MANOR

This was the home of another Quaker family – that of James Douglas, whose son John became known as 'honest John'. What a marvellous title to have in business! He lived at Landscape Manor, where De La Salle College stands today. He had his business at 17/18 Wexford Street. It is said that he kept the people of the city fed during the 1916 Rising, by bringing produce in from Landscape Manor. James Douglas came from Lurgan, County Armagh, where his brother had set up

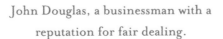
John Douglas, a businessman with a reputation for fair dealing.

an industrial school for deprived children; this afforded John a steady supply of good, honest labour for his shop. At one time he had twenty-two past pupils as apprentices. Before his death in 1894, James requested that Landscape Manor be turned into a house of industry for deprived children of dublin, like his brother's school in Lurgan. It is not clear exactly why his wishes were not adhered to, but it took eighty years to execute the will. His brother Jacob ran a business in Capel Street.

John's daughter Isobel (1892–1977) trained as a Fröebel teacher, and opened Rathgar Junior School on Grosvenor Road, which is still operating today. Isobel was imbued with the Celtic Revival spirit of the time, and went to Ring in County Waterford to learn Irish.

Among Douglas's other offspring was James Green Douglas (1887–1954). A self-educated man, he was appointed by Michael Collins as chairman of the committee to draft an Irish constitution.

As a member of the Irish White Cross, established in 1921 to distribute American aid money, he had huge influence in raising money from his fellow Quakers in the United States. He was vice-chairman of the first Senate in 1922. The Senate was abolished in 1936, but was reconstituted in 1938, and he again became a senator until 1944. James Green Douglas died in 1954, and was buried in the Religious Society of Friends cemetery at Temple Hill, Blackrock, County Dublin.

David Pedlow also lived at Landscape Manor. Pedlow also came from Lurgan, and was the farm manager, taking over the farm on the death of John Douglas. The Royal Dublin Society lists show Pedlow to be one of the most progressive farmers in south County Dublin, with numerous gold medals won both for his horses and shorthorn dairy herd. Pedlow vied with his neighbours, the Hughes Brothers, as to who had the best herd. Kieran Fagan states in his book *The Story of HB* (2006) that, were it not for Pedlow's untimely death in 1915, we could all be eating Pedlow ice cream today. When testing was introduced to standardise the quality of milk, only the milk of Hughes Brothers and Pedlow was described as 'rich' in the south County Dublin area.

The drag hunt, where a scent is laid out and the huntsmen and hounds follow it, used to leave on Saturdays from the yard of Landscape Manor. It is difficult to imagine a hunt of any kind taking place in the area now!

OTHER HOUSES IN CHURCHTOWN

Camberley Oaks was built in the late 1700s. It has had several names, including Barren or Barn Elms, Camberley and Inish Ealga. Barn Elms is now an industrial estate further up the road. The name Camberley came from Reverend Matthew Campbell, who was a curate of Taney church (1787–1814). Amelia Ffrench ran a select Catholic boarding school in the house when it was called Barn Elms, in the 1880s.

Perhaps the most interesting owner of Camberley Oaks was Áine Ceannt. She was the widow of Éamonn Ceannt, who was one of the signatories of the 1916 Proclamation. Although left a widow with a son, she was no shrinking violet. She was a District Justice in the Republican Courts in Rathmines during the War of Independence. These courts were set up to try to keep law and order in the country, in defiance of British rule.

The 1916 Rising, the War of Independence and the Great War in Europe all took place within ten years. To put it mildly, the country was in ruins. Around this time, a group of individuals came together to see what could be done to alleviate the suffering of women and children. Áine Ceannt, along with Laurence O'Neill, then Lord Mayor of Dublin, set up the Irish White Cross fund. They gathered a group around them of all political and religious shades.

In the United States, word had spread that things were bad in Ireland. Remember, we are talking about first-generation Irish emigrants then. The Committee for the Relief of Irish Distress was set up in 1917.

The Committee raised $5 million – a huge amount for that time. The Committee consisted of R. Barclay; Spicer and William Price, Philadelphia; B. Wilber, Greenwich, New York; and John Barker and Walter Longstroth, Pennsylvania. All of these Quaker gentlemen visited Ireland between January and April 1921. In consultation with them, Mrs Ceannt set up a fund that was generally administered through the parish priests of the country. This had its good and bad sides, as local knowledge is one thing, but local prejudice is another. Áine Ceannt was the chief administrator of the Irish White Cross fund, and she travelled all over the country in that capacity. Mr J.H. Webb, whose father was a member of Isaac Butt's first Home Rule Committee, was chairman, and he held that position for twenty-two years. He was an architect by profession, and a commissioner in St John's Ambulance. The Irish White Cross ceased its activities in the 1940s.

Mrs Ceannt lived in Inish Ealga until 1949. Then the De La Salle community purchased it, first as a house for the community and then as a private junior school. Mrs Ceannt and her son moved to the gate lodge, to the right of the Camberley estate.

Braemor Road

The name Braemor is derived from the names of the two builders, Mr K. Brady and Mr F. Morton: *Bra* for Brady, *Mor* for Morton, and *E* for Brady's wife Etheline. This building partnership was formed before the Second World War to build luxurious houses, namely Braemor Park.

So the original Churchtown Road, now basically Churchtown Road Upper, came from Dundrum, ran left at the green and continued on, turning right into what is now Landscape Road, then left and down the hill. Where the road reached the Dodder, Ely Arch would have been on your left-hand side.

To return to the green: Between Airfield House and the former Braemor Rooms pub, there is a lane known as Airfield Park, on the corner that used be known as Field's Corner. Field was a landowner in the area in the early 1800s. In the 1950s, it was known as Young's Corner, after the family who owned the shop there. The lane forms part of the county boundary, as well as the ancient parish boundary between Taney and Rathfarnham. The boundary crosses the road here, goes through the houses and on to the Milltown golf course. The stream that marked the boundary is culverted here, covered with concrete.

St Nathy's House apartment block, on the corner of Beaumont Avenue and Upper Churchtown Road, again derives its name from the little church. This is built on the site of Westin or Weston House.

In the 1920s, a Mrs Buckley lived in Briar's Cottage on the opposite side of Upper Churchtown Road, and ran a small dairy from there. Beaumont Avenue was known as Nowlan's Avenue, Nowlan being a property owner in the area in the 1800s. According to Jim Nolan's book *Changing Faces* (1982), the field at the far end of the avenue, where Barton Road is now, was known as Free

Enderly House, built around 1866, is built on the site of an earlier house called Sweet Mount.
It is currently under renovation.

State Field. The army of Saorstát Éireann, or the Free State, was billeted here before the British Army evacuated the barracks in 1922. During that time, the area was frequented by ladies of the night, and became known as Piccadilly.

BEAUMONT AVENUE

The Bottle Tower pub gets its name from the Bottle Tower folly, located on Whitehall Road.

Mountain View was the family home of the Cosgraves. They owned land in the area, and had butcher's shops. One of the sons, Jack, had a pig farm at Barn Elms. His sons are the well-known builders Cosgrave Brothers, who have been large property developers in Dublin over the last thirty years.

Belfield House, built in 1720, is one of the oldest houses in the area.

At the top of the road on Sweetmount Avenue, hidden away, is a house called **Enderley**. Built around 1886, it is being totally refurbished at the moment.

Barn Elms is now an industrial estate, but it used to be the 'pound', where wandering animals were taken if found straying on the roads. This was run by Jack Cosgrave. Another Cosgrave brother, Phil, delivered milk. In ancient times, the pounds were run by the church vestries of parish churches as a money-making enterprise. Taney Parish in Dundrum had one of these pounds.

Airfield House was once called Sarahfield. Patrick A. Conway, an ex-Head Constable, lived there in the 1890s.

On the other side of Churchtown Road is Briarly, where David Pedlow lived before he moved into Landscape Manor.

Belfield House is one of the oldest houses in Churchtown, dating from around 1720. Over the years, it has had a number of owners; one of the more interesting was John McKenny, a proprietor of Vitriol Works in Ballybough. The Vitriol Works, which produced sulphuric acid, are mentioned in Joyce's short story 'An Encounter'.

Belfield Terrace was built on the lands of Belfield House. Number 3 was the home of the Yeats sisters, and was called Gurteen Dhas.

Churchtown Park was built around 1850. In the 1860s, it was occupied by Charles Malone's brother Isaac. The Johnson family, who ran a business on Ormond Quay, lived here from 1864 to 1905. The house is now split into apartments. All of the houses down as far as Woodville are built on the land of Churchtown Park.

Woodville was occupied by another Quaker, the opthalmic surgeon Dr Arthur Jacob, in about 1875. Another resident of the house was Fred Switzer, a Palatine whose family originally came from southern Germany. He owned Switzers department store in Grafton Street, which has now become Brown Thomas. Methodist historian Reverend D.A. Levistone Cooney tells the story that during the War of Independence, the IRA came to blow up the house. Switzer woke and, opening the window armed with a large dinner gong, beat it strongly. The IRA men, taking this as a signal to the local RIC station, fled, and the house was spared. Remember, in the 1920s, County Dublin at night would have been virtually silent.

Switzer's wife was Florence Mary Riggs, related to Bobby Riggs, the Wimbledon tennis champion who won the singles, doubles and mixed doubles titles in 1939. Florence ran a

Ardtona on Lower Churchtown Road, a private school since 1941.

very successful restaurant in aid of the Red Cross during the First World War. Called 'Bonne Bouche', it was located first in Dawson Street, and then moved to Grafton Street. Of course, when Switzers opened a restaurant in their shop, it was supplied with milk from the Jersey herd kept at Woodville. This house was originally chosen by the De La Salle brothers as a school premises, but Archbishop John Charles McQuaid felt it was unseemly to have a boys' school so close to a convent school.

LOWER CHURCHTOWN ROAD

Ardtona was originally called Lyndhurst, but was renamed around 1875, when a John Hobbs Peart acquired it. He had another residence in County Kildare. The house had two entrances – the current entrance and another on the corner of Upper Churchtown Road.

An interesting man arrived to this house around 1912. He was a Corkman called Ignatius O'Brien. A barrister, he had made his name in an odd case in Youghal in the 1880s. A local priest, Canon Keller, was subpoenaed as a witness in a bankruptcy case. Keller stated that the information he had was obtained in the confessional box, and so he would not divulge it. He was found guilty of contempt of court. But O'Brien appealed the case, and Keller was acquitted. At that time, there were several examples of priests being prosecuted like this. O'Brien became Lord Chancellor of the Exchequer Court, one of the Four Courts in Dublin. He took the name Lord Shandon.

During the 1916 Rising, the War of Independence and the Civil War, Lord Shandon was regarded as being on the side of the Government. Although Ardtona was protected by the Royal Irish Constabulary, he was threatened and later burnt out. He decided to leave Ireland, and fled to England in 1922, where he died in 1931.

The next owner of Ardtona was a Mrs Nash, who ran a tennis club here in 1924. She gradually sold off plots of land for development.

In October 1941, at the request of a Father Riordan, a curate in Dundrum, a private school was started at Ardtona by Mrs S.H. Rogerson. This was a brave decision, given that it was in the middle of the Second World War. The school still flourishes today, and it is known as Ardtona House. It was then in the Dundrum Parish, until 1957, when the parish of Churchtown was founded.

Above: Palmerston Park, landscaped by William Sheppard.

Below: Moyola House, 74 Lower Churchtown Road.

Charleville was the home of William Sheppard (1842–1923), a renowned landscape gardener. He supervised the work on St Stephen's Green for Lord Ardilaun (1880). He also landscaped the green in Harold's Cross, as well as Palmerston Park. Sheppard's landscaping generally included a feature waterfall on each of his sites. After leaving Charleville, he went to live at 79 Kenilworth Square. There is a memorial in St Patrick's Cathedral to William Sheppard's wife, Jemima Tiller – what an appropriate name for a gardener's wife!

Then John Christopher Fitzachary took up residence. His book *The Bridal of Drimna* (1883) is an amusing collection of poetry, complete with a nice mention of the Dodder:

> *Then on the Dodder gazing*
> *With unutterable glee*
> *I would coin, with power amazing*
> *Full many a simile.*

Number 100 Churchtown Road Lower, which housed Lily and Lolly Yeats's Cuala Industries.

Moyola House derives its name from an area near Castledawson, County Derry. The land on which Moyola House stands, measuring nearly two acres, was granted a lease in 1862. The first mention of Moyola in *Thom's Dublin Directory* is in 1889, when James Wellington Pepper owned it. He donated a prize to the Royal Horticultural Society.

Several people owned it after that. Around the 1940s, Mr and Mrs Brady bought it. The builders of Braemor Park appeared to part company in the late 1940s. Mr Brady built Woodlawn Park. As you can still see, this was an exclusive bungalow development. However, in the sale of these bungalows, one restriction was imposed by Mr Brady – he would not sell to a Roman Catholic. This may appear odd, but I have come across another area in Terenure with the same restriction. When Mr Brady died, his wife continued to live there until the 1960s. It was then sold and the lands around it were developed into Moyola Court in 1971.

Opposite Moyola is a little cottage, 100 Lower Churchtown Road. If only the walls of that place could talk! In this house, the Yeats sisters, Lily and Lolly, ran the Cuala Press. James Joyce mentions them in *Ulysses*:

Five lines of text and ten pages of notes about the folk and the fishgods of Dundrum.
Printed by the weird sisters in the year of the big wind.

Joyce was a bit harsh on them.

The Yeats family came from Sligo. Their father John studied law, but never practised, instead becoming an illustrator and portrait painter. He married Susan Pollexfen (1841–1900). Now, as you can imagine, there wasn't a lot of work for a portrait painter in Dublin, so the family emigrated to London in 1887. Their first child, Susan, who was known as Lily, was born on 25 August 1866; and Elizabeth, known as Lolly, on 11 March 1868. Their brother William B. was born on 13 June 1865, and Jack B. on 29 August 1871.

The whole family were artistic. While in London, Lily went to work with May Morris, daughter of famous socialist and designer William Morris, regarded as the founder of the Arts and Crafts movement. Lily worked mainly at embroidery at Morris's home, Kelmscott House. Meanwhile, Lolly learned the art of editing.

Some of the beautiful output of Cuala Industries,
in tapestry and in print.

The Yeats family returned to Ireland, living first on Upper Churchtown Road. But with all the art in the family, times were tough. Filled with Irish Literary Revival spirit, Evelyn Gleeson and the Yeats sisters set up Dun Emer Industries at Runnymede, Dundrum, which they renamed Dun Emer. They specialised in tapestries and printing. That partnership split after a few years, mainly due to money matters, with Evelyn feeling she was the main source of income. In 1908, the Yeats sisters set up Cuala Industries, and moved to 'Gurteen Dhas', a cottage on Lower Churchtown Road. Around this time, their mother became reclusive due to illness, and eventually died. Their father chose to go into exile, and went to live in the United States.

Money was a constant worry. William Butler, the poet, was earning some money from royalties, but not a lot. At Cuala Industries, Lily produced beautiful works of embroidery, while Lolly ran the publishing press. W.B. Yeats, editor-in-chief, was never happy with anything produced, and there were constant rows. Lily, although the eldest, didn't like arguments or confrontation, while Lolly was bossier and more dominant. She was a workaholic, and expected everybody else to be the same. By all accounts, she was cranky and hard to deal with. As time went on, the relationship between the two sisters deteriorated, like a bad marriage.

They produced W.B.'s books, and also those by other authors. The first book they published, on 8 October 1908, was *Poetry and Ireland* by W.B. Yeats and Lionel Johnson. Along with books, they published a series of 'broadsides'. The first was published in June 1908, and the series continued monthly for seven years. Each one was in folio format measuring 11x7½ inches, printed on paper made at Saggart Mill. Broadsides were printed on pages 1, 2 and 3, while page 4 was blank. A complete series of the original broadsides is worth a fortune now.

The cottage was at the hub of the Irish Literary Revival, with George Russell, John Millington Synge, Oliver St John Gogarty, Frank O'Connor and Padraic Colum among the authors published here. Jack B. Yeats, Victor Brown, Beatrice Elvery (Lady Glenavy), Harry Kernoff and Maurice McGonigal, among others, illustrated the broadsides. The battles over the editing and illustrations were renowned.

Lolly had a relationship of sorts with Louis Purser. She felt they were going to marry, but they never did. Louis was appointed professor of Latin at Trinity College in 1897, and was regarded as one of the great classical scholars. Some said that it was because she was 'crossed in love' that Lolly was so contrary.

Louis's sister Sarah Purser (1848–1943) formed the stained glass co-operative works An Túr Gloine. Sarah was also imbued with the revivalist spirit, and would have been friends with the Yeats family.

Lolly was also an excellent art teacher. Trained as a Fröebel teacher, she taught art in a number of schools. She wrote a paper on painting entitled 'Why brushwork should be included in all kindergarten time tables'. She taught Louis le Brocquy and Mainie Jellett as children in a small school in Palmerston Road called Mount Temple Kindergarten.

An advertisement for Cuala Press stated that it was only a short walk from the tram stop to their premises in Churchtown. The tram stop was in Dartry, a distance of over a mile. Years ago people didn't mind walking.

The lease expired on the cottage in Churchtown, so, in 1923, Cuala Press moved into W.B. Yeats's house at 82 Merrion Square. In 1925, they transferred to 133 Baggot Street, and finally on to 46 Palmerston Road, Rathmines, where W.B.'s widow, Georgie, resided. They had married when Georgie was twenty-five and W.B. was fifty-two. He proposed to her just weeks after Iseult Gonne had rejected him.

The Yeats sisters attended St Nahi's church, Dundrum, and there are marvellous examples of Lily's embroideries in the church. The Yeats sisters also embroidered the vestments for the Eucharistic Congress in 1932.

Another example of the Yeats sisters' work is in Loughrea Cathedral, County Galway, along with early works from An Túr Gloine. Lolly died on 16 January 1940. Lily died on 5 January 1949, not having worked for some time. The sisters are buried together in St Nahi's cemetery, Dundrum.

Top: The graveyard at St Nahi's Church.
Right: Evie Hone, an experimental Irish painter and stained glass artist.

Another artist associated with St Nahi's church is Evie Hone (1894–1955). Hone had been a member of the Church of Ireland, and lived with her family in Stillorgan. Her father was Governor of the Bank of Ireland. Evie contracted polio when she was eleven years old, but never let this inhibit her. In 1937, she became a convert to Roman Catholicism, after which her work took on a more religious tone.

As well as a beautiful stained glass window in St Nahi's, examples of her work can be seen in Clongowes Wood, Blackrock, Eton College in England and in the new Cathedral of Washington DC. Hone was in the vanguard of Irish women painters, having first gone to London and then on to Paris with Mainie Jellett, where they studied under André Lhote and later Albert Gleizes, a pioneer of cubism. Hone and Jellett were among the first Irish painters to embrace modernism. When Evie died in 1954, she was buried in St Maelruain's cemetery, Tallaght.

Continuing on Lower Churchtown Road

Beyond the Quaker meeting house is a group of buildings known as the ex-servicemen houses. The proper name of this housing scheme is the Irish Sailors and Soldiers Land Trust. The Trust was set up under the Irish Land Bill, which received royal assent in 1919. It was designed to form distinct communities of loyal ex-servicemen, and the bill stipulated that it was only open to citizens who had been loyal during the War. In all, the Trust built over 3,000 houses

Insidious recruiting advertisements for the First World War.

throughout Ireland, Killester Garden Village being one of the biggest schemes. The houses on Lower Churchtown Road were built in 1929, and the Trust remained in operation until 1987, when it was dissolved. One of the great speeches regarding the First World War was delivered by Senator Maurice Manning at the winding up of the Trust:

Irishmen who went off to fight in the First World War were the forgotten and excluded men who escaped poverty and the lack of opportunity at home. Heeding the appeals of John Redmond and John Dillon, that Ireland's participation in the War and a victory for the British forces would result in the speedy granting of Home Rule for all Ireland, or those like Tom Kettle and others, who believed they were fighting for the freedom of small nations. One could not rule out that in many cases, people went to join the Great War out of a sense of adventure. They were certainly as Irish as anybody else, and yet they seemed to be excluded in some strange way from the nationalist orthodoxy.

Lord Killanin was the last Chairman, and when the Trust was wound up it was still in funds. So now, way ahead of any peace agreement between northern and southern Ireland, Lord Killanin and the governments of Ireland and the United Kingdom decided that the money should be spent on cross-border projects. One of the projects they chose was the Lough Erne Canal, which they made navigable.

Just past these houses, opposite the entrance to Milltown Golf Club, is a house called Loreto, where the film actress Maureen O'Hara (1920–2015) was reared.

CLASSON'S BRIDGE

The next time you cross the Dodder at the Dropping Well pub, if you look closely you will see a plaque with the inscription 'Classon's Bridge'. So, who was Classon?

In the late 1800s, John Classon had a saw mill in Milltown. He lived in a townhouse in Eustace Street, but his principal residence was an estate in Newtownmountkennedy, County Wicklow. One day, while travelling from Wicklow, his horse bolted and he was thrown from his carriage. He was severely injured, and unable to work again, and his business gradually suffered until finally he lost everything.

His son, also John Classon, was born into that wealthy family, but with the decline in their fortunes, he was educated in 'a cheap school in Yorkshire', where he claimed they weren't even fed. John's sister Eliza had to work as a governess. One of the families she worked for was that of Archibald Hamilton, father of William Rowan Hamilton, one of the world's most renowned mathematicians, who discovered quaternions. Rowan Hamilton was on tour in America at the time Eliza was governess to his family.

When we look at Taylor's map of 1815, we see that there was a bridge spanning the Dodder, but prior to 1800, the road did not go up to Churchtown. Why put a bridge there at all? Well, at the time there were several mills on the Dodder, as well as a quarry and a gravel pit, so access was needed.

The bridge is a three-span, arched construction, made of limestone. There were limestone quarries all over south County Dublin at that time, in Rathgar, Terenure, Dundrum and, perhaps most importantly, Milltown. Just down from the Nine Arches Bridge was the quarry that was used to rebuild the walls of Christ Church Cathedral, after the roof and much of the south side of the cathedral collapsed in 1562.

Classon's Bridge is very similar to Pack Horse Bridge, just downstream. It was always in dreadful condition, as this 1897 letter from John Christopher Fitzachary to *The Irish Times* states:

This primate and dangerous structure is so narrow that it only admits of the passing of a single vehicle at a time, and the pedestrian who then happens to be crossing runs a good chance of being knocked down or jammed against the parapets on either side. There are a couple of refuge niches in one of the walls, but they are generally in such a filthy state, that few, indeed would care to avail themselves of them ...

In 1819, John Classon ran a farming implement factory at 2 Blackhall Place. It supplied ploughs, seed harrows, Dutch sowing machines and one- and two-horse threshing machines, the latter of which could thresh sixty to eighty barrels a day! John Watson Stewart's *The Gentleman's and Citizen's Almanack* of 1812 states that Classon and Duggan (iron merchants) traded at 39 Bridgefoot St. This company went on to trade in timber, iron, steel and tinplate.

John Classon was also an agent for Nine Elms, London, who exported Roman cement, and for the Penbryn Slate Company at 18 Eden Quay. He became one of the great agricultural innovators of the early nineteenth century. Classon was a member of the RDS from 1809 to 1860. In 1828, he argued strongly that better merchantable quality and therefore a better price for hay could be attained by bringing it to market in tied trusses, rather than the traditional loose load.

Classon, like a lot of successful businessmen, started to invest in other enterprises. One of these investments was in the building of the Northumberland Hotel in Beresford Place, and next door to it a music hall that seated 4,000 people. The hotel became the headquarters of the Irish Transport and General Workers Union (ITGWU), and was renamed Liberty Hall. The 1916 Proclamation of the Republic was printed in this building. It was also where the insurrectionists assembled before marching to the GPO on Easter Monday, 1916.

Classon lived in Fairfield House, Rathgar. He died in 1868, and is buried in Mount Jerome Cemetery, Harold's Cross.

Just beside Classon's Bridge is an entrance to a laneway through Milltown Golf Club. The name Riversdale House is on the gatepost. To get a picture of IRA activities on this laneway, we are lucky to have the testimony of Patrick Brennan.

Patrick Brennan lived in Lower Churchtown Road, and was a member of the Irish Volunteers. After the 1916 Rising, he joined the IRA. The Sixth Battalion controlled south County Dublin, and its main function was to create diversions, to lead the forces of the Crown away from the city centre. In the years leading up to the Civil War, there were constant skirmishes in the area, and one of the main targets was Classon's Bridge. The IRA put roadblocks at the Nine Arches Bridge, at Dartry Dye Works and on Lower Churchtown Road, and they tried several times to blow up the bridge. During one attempt, the British got to within fifty yards of the bridge, and two or possibly three British soldiers were killed. One Volunteer was severely wounded. After four unsuccessful attempts, the bridge was finally blown up in June 1921.

A holy water font in Milltown Parish church
dedicated to Patrick Doyle.

A Dartry Dye Works van, advertising 'Drytex Cleaning'.

Dartry Dye Works used to dye the tunics of the Black and Tans. The IRA raided the premises, gathered the tunics together, and set them alight. The British were alerted, but the IRA made their escape, crossing the Dodder and coming down the lane here. The Dublin Laundry was also raided by the IRA, because the uniforms of the RIC were laundered there.

British soldiers stationed in Rathmines would meet their girlfriends and take the number 14 tram to its terminus in Dartry. They would walk from there to the lane to find a secluded 'courting spot' on the banks of the Dodder. On several occasions in the early months of 1921, the IRA captured a group of soldiers, and ordered them to divest themselves, except for their shirts and trousers. Brennan states that the soldiers were involved in intelligence work. I think they may have had other things on their minds.

DODDER WATERFALL, RATHMINES, DUBLIN.

An idyllic place for a stroll, by the weir on the Dodder (not in Rathmines, as the postcard states).

PATRICK DOYLE ROAD

Patrick (Paddy) Doyle was born and lived in Milltown. He was married to Sarah, and had five children. On the day Paddy was killed in 1916, their youngest child, Joe, was a year old. Sarah's other children were Paddy (fourteen), Molly (twelve), Jack (seven) and Charlie (four). She cared for them all, but in 1919, Charlie, who was in the company of a neighbour's child, sitting on a bridge spanning the Dodder, fell in and was killed. Then in 1922, her eldest son Paddy, having joined the Free State Army, was killed in an ambush in Crooksling, County Dublin.

Her only daughter Molly died in childbirth in 1940, leaving five children. Sarah took that family in, and two of the children remained with her. In the 1940s, her son Joe was interned in 'Tintown' in the Curragh, having been caught in possession of a gun. Sarah also looked after her brother Mike, who had been invalided out of the Royal Irish Fusiliers and had fought in the Great War.

Sarah was renowned in Milltown as nurse, cook and counsellor, not only to her family, but also to the community in general. They lived in Millmount, Rosy Hill, Milltown. I am grateful to May Nolan, Molly's daughter, for a letter and family photos.

Paddy Doyle was a devout Catholic, attending Mass daily in Milltown church. He earned his living as a manager in the Dublin Laundry. Doyle was an IRB Volunteer, and a musketry instructor in the Third Battalion.

On Easter Monday morning, 1916, Doyle was on his way to Liberty Hall, but he met a couple of men who advised him to go to Boland's Mills. While there, he was commanded to go to Clanwilliam House.

The garrison in Clanwilliam House was seven. There were other volunteers in the parochial hall, diagonally opposite, and also in 25 Northumberland Road, but the total was only thirteen Volunteers. George Reynolds, Patrick Doyle, Richard Murphy, James Doyle (no relation), Willie Ronan and Tom and James Walsh were the men in Clanwilliam House.

Their arms and ammunition consisted of four Lee Enfield rifles, two Martini rifles, two Mausers (Howth guns), two .38 revolvers, two .45 revolvers, one .38 automatic revolver and about 2,000 rounds of ammunition. This was to defend one of the most strategic areas in the city. While in Clanwilliam House, the Volunteers discovered a load of coal in the basement. They proceeded to fill sacks, bringing the coal upstairs to barricade the windows.

The Volunteers defended their position against the Georgius Rex Regiment (aka God's Rejected and Gorgeous Wrecks). Reinforcements were ordered to the area, and the Seventh and Eighth battalions of the Sherwood Foresters now marched on Clanwilliam House. The Volunteers were overwhelmed, and Clanwilliam House became an inferno. The coal that had acted as barricades now became fuel for the fire.

A witness stated: 'At one point Patrick Doyle suddenly stopped firing and spoke no more; he was an inveterate talker and when one of the Walshes shook him he fell over.' (*Dublin in Rebellion* by J.E.A. Connell Jnr) As well as Paddy Doyle, two other Volunteers were killed – George Reynolds and Dick Murphy. The bodies of the three fallen Volunteers were never recovered; they were cremated in the fire.

Official reports state that four officers were killed, with fourteen wounded. Two hundred and sixteen British soldiers were either killed or wounded in the area. Among the British officers killed was F.H. Browning, who in 1914 had formed the 'Pals', a company of the Royal Dublin Fusiliers composed of volunteers from the Irish Rugby Football Union (IRFU). He was President of the IRFU, and had been an outstanding rugby and cricket player. He had been returning with his Regiment from manoeuvres in the Dublin Mountains when they were called to the action at Clanwilliam House.

In addition to having a road named after him, Paddy Doyle is commemorated in Milltown church by an inscription on the holy water font. He is acknowledged on a gravestone in St Nahi's graveyard, where his son Paddy is buried.

MILLTOWN GOLF CLUB

In Dublin in the early 1900s, several golf clubs were founded. Portmarnock and Royal Dublin were already established. In 1907, a group of men got together and decided to set up a golf course here in Milltown. The 'drive in' was on 28 September of that year. At first, they had thirty-seven acres, but later they acquired more land, and Milltown Golf Club now has about ninety acres.

Milltown Golf Course, with the club house in the distance.

The club started with nine holes, but now has eighteen. The first president of the club was William Martin Murphy (1844–1919), who lived just over the road in Dartry House, Orwell Park.

There were few people in Dublin at that with time more sway than William Martin Murphy. He was among the most influential businessmen in the city, owning the Dublin United Tramways Company, Independent Newspapers and Clery's Department Store. Nor did he restrict his business interests to Ireland – he built railways in England, South America and on the Gold Coast of west Africa. Originally from Bantry, County Cork, the Murphy family moved to Dublin and William was educated at Belvedere College. When, on the death of his father, he took over the family building business, he was only nineteen.

Murphy was elected a Nationalist Member of Parliament for St Patrick's Ward, Dublin, from 1885 to 1892. Although disillusioned with nationalist politics, he refused a knighthood from King Edward VII in 1906. Of course, he is best remembered for leading the employers of Dublin against the trade unions in the confrontation that led to the lockout of 1913.

Murphy was President of Milltown Golf Club from 1907 until his death in 1919. He was succeeded as President by Lord Justice O'Connor (1919–1924), followed by J.B. Moore (1924–1928) and then by Murphy's son, Dr William Lombard Murphy (Lombard coming from his mother's maiden name), from 1928 to 1943.

William Lombard Murphy was an ear, nose and throat surgeon at St Vincent's Hospital, Dublin, and served in the Royal Army Medical Corps during the First World War. Being a linguist and stationed in Salonika, Murphy became a Liaison Officer between British, French and Serbian medical units. Among his awards were Le Croix de Guerre, the Chevalier of the Legion of Honour, the Serbian Order of St Sava and the Greek Order of the Redeemer. He represented Saorstát Éireann at the 1929 and 1930 international labour conferences in Geneva.

Dr Murphy continued his father's business interests, and was also a patron of the Feis Ceol and the Rathmines & Rathgar Musical Society. When he died in 1943, he left an estate of £150,000, which included a legacy to Dr Oliver Chance, a pioneering cancer specialist.

Milltown Golf Club has been home to golfers of all standards, from high-ranking professionals to the enthusiasts that keep Titleist executives in the luxury to which they have become accustomed. What is less well-known is that its members have included patriots, some of whom fought for their king and some for the Republic. It may be confusing, but yes, among the membership were people who fought for King, and some for freedom from the King.

Milltown Golf Club's roll of honour of members then serving with 'His Majesty's Forces', August 1914.

These words were penned by a former Milltown member:

The Lost Ball

Playing one day at the seaside,

I was topping my balls on the tees,

And the sand and the bent were littered

With fragments of double Ds;

Piffle supreme I was playing,

And varying 'slice' with 'pull',

But I hit one ball a wallop

Like a kick of a Spanish bull

['Double Ds' are golf balls.]

These words were written by the same member:

So here, while mad guns curse overhead,

And tired men sigh with mud for couch and floor,

Know that we fools, now with the foolish dead,

Died not for flag, nor King, nor Emperor,

But for a dream, born in a herdsman's shed,

And for the secret Scripture of the poor.

[Written before Guillemont, Somme, 4 September 1916]

Both of these poems were written by T.M. Kettle (1880–1916), poet, essayist, politician and first Professor of Economics in UCD, whose bust by Albert Power is in St Stephen's Green.

Kettle was born on 9 February 1880, in Artane, County Dublin. His father was a renowned Parnellite and among the founders of the Land League. He was also a wealthy farmer. Kettle started his education in the Christian Brothers School in North Richmond Street, and then went to Clongowes Wood College.

He then attended the Royal/Catholic University (later to become University College, Dublin). It was a college in name only, with few facilities, and students would often use the facilities of the National Library. Here he joined the Literary and Historical Society, and became its auditor for the period 1898–99. Among Kettle's friends were James Joyce, Oliver St John Gogarty and Francis Sheehy-Skeffington.

David Sheehy MP (Kettle's future father-in-law) lived at 2 Belvedere Place, with his wife, two sons and four daughters. Both Kettle and Joyce fell for the youngest of the daughters, Mary. Kettle and Joyce had also attended the same schools, but not at the same time.

Kettle, after finishing his degree, went to the King's Inns to study law. He was called to the bar in 1905, but never practised. The following year, he became a Member of Parliament for East Tyrone, a seat he held until he resigned in 1910. In 1909, he married Mary Sheehy, and became Professor of Economics at University College, Dublin. Kettle was Chairman of the Peace Committee that tried to bring an end to the Dublin Strike of 1913. Here, of course, he would have been in contact with fellow club member William Martin Murphy.

Kettle joined the 'Dubs' – the Royal Dublin Fusiliers – in 1914, as a Lieutenant. He was sent to the front that same year. He survived his first tour and came back to Ireland. After the Rising of 1916, which upset and affected him deeply, he returned to the front. He was killed at the Somme on 9 September 1916, one of forty million to lose their lives in that war.

In *Milltown Golf Club: An illustrated centenary history*, it is stated that in 1916, a cheque was presented to the British Red Cross, following an open mixed foursomes competition. A lot of outings were held either to raise funds or to give recovering wounded soldiers a day out.

Sadly, this parchment appears to be the only recognition of members who participated in the First World War. The above parchment was offered to Milltown Golf Club to display, prior to the publication of their centenary book, but this offer was declined.

Until 1937, Orwell Road was known as Dodder Road from the junction of Lower Churchtown Road to the River Dodder. At the end of the golf course, there is a lane that I mentioned earlier in relation to Classon's Bridge near the Dropping Well. A stream runs beside the lane; it continues up Orwell Road and through the southern side of Milltown Golf Club, now mostly culverted. That is the old boundary between the Taney and Rathfarnham parishes, part of

The gravestone of Francis Lawlor, or
Frainnc Ó Leathlobhair, a Dublin Brigade
IRA Volunteer shot in the nearby lane.

i n-ðil ċuimne aṛ
ṛṛainnc ó leaṫlobaiṛ
(LAWLOR)
ceann ṛanᴣa coṁluċt ð
an tṛeaṛ cat
bṛioᴣaið aṫa cliaṫ
ð'aṛm na poblacta
a ðunṁ aṛbuiᴣcað
aṛ an laṫaiṛ ṛeo
29ᵃᵈ mi na noðlaiᴣ 1922
ERECTED BY THE NATIONAL GRAVES ASSOCIATION
R. I. P.

the boundary I mentioned earlier when I was referring to the lane next to the Braemor Rooms. So it is
fair to say that this lane dates back to Norman times,
i.e. the eleventh or twelfth century, when the parish
system was set up. This boundary was later used as
the county boundary.

At the entrance to this laneway on Orwell Road,
there is a memorial erected by the National Graves
Association. This is to the memory of Francis Lawlor, who was a member of D Company, 3rd Battalion Dublin Brigade IRA. Lawlor was the son of a Dublin Metropolitan Policeman, and fought
in the War of Independence. Unmarried and aged thirty in 1922, he lived at 3 Raglan Road, and
was employed as an auditor.

On 28 December of that year, Lawlor was taken from 6 Castlewood Avenue, Rathmines,
where he was visiting, and the following morning his body was found by a man cycling to work.
The Freeman's Journal gives an account of the grim scene:

When discovered the victim was lying in the middle of the laneway, on his back, with his hands
across his breast about ten paces from the main road.

There were two entrance bullet holes in the right side of the head and two exit wounds in the
left hand side of the head and marks of other wounds in the body.

Beside the deceased was a large pool of blood, and although no expended cartridges were
found in the vicinity, it would appear the body was shot where it lay.

It was thought that the killing was carried out by men from Oriel House, the Intelligence unit
of Saorstát Éireann. This is how it was during the Civil War.

Judge Chair Davitt, in his testimony in the military archives on the killing of Frank Lawlor,
states that 'the killing had all the appearance of being an unofficial execution carried out by
government forces'.

Dartry Cottages, close to the
Dodder, built for mill workers.

The lane was mostly used at night, by courting couples. It was known by several different names – Lovers' Lane, Green Lane, Tinker's Lane and Lambert's Lane. Lambert was a farmer who had the right of way to use the lane to water his cattle.

CONTINUING ALONG ORWELL ROAD – GREEN PARK

The name seems to derive from the name of the laneway. The houses which stand here now were built in the 1920s and 1930s, by John Kenny and Sons of Harcourt Street. The architect was Rupert Jones. The estate was built on the lands of Errigal House, which is now the Russian Embassy.

Green Park was an estate for the upper middle class who wished to live in the country and could afford to do so. An estate agent's brochure describes Green Park as set in 'lovely surroundings, sea and mountain air'. It adds that 'all plumbing will be copper and there will be an ample

The entrance lodge at the Russian Embassy
on Orwell Road,

supply of hot water. A proportion of the windows will be glazed with Vita Glass which passes the ultra violet rays and gives the equivalent of sunshine in the home.'

The houses were expensive, ranging from £2,150 to £2,475 in 1929. Kenny went on to build the Mount Merrion estate. He grazed cattle on the site as he was building the houses, so nothing was wasted.

Errigal House was built in the 1890s by a barrister called Wilson. Then John Boydell bought it. He was a malster and corn merchant, and incidentally, in 1913, his house was connected to one of the first telephone lines in Dublin. The number was Rathfarnham 8. He was a church warden for the Rathfarnham parish.

Boydell was also a member of the Dublin Chamber of Commerce. But in the autumn of 1921, again during the War of Independence, he was burnt out. The house was empty for several years, and was then restored by a professor of experimental physics at Trinity College, namely William Edmund Thrift. I presume he funded the restoration by the sale of the nine acres on which the estate, Green Park was built. Looking at the house now, you can see the lovely granite wall and railings.

John Kinahan and his family moved into Errigal House. The Kinahans owned a chain of confectionery shops all over Dublin. There seem to have been seventeen in all. The Kinahan business was sold off in the early 1970s.

The house was then sold to the Irish Management Institute, who had its headquarters here from 5 April 1974 to 10 September 1983. The USSR Government then bought it. I remember there was always a garda on duty outside the embassy throughout the 1980s and early 1990s, but that service came to a sudden end in the late 1990s.

ARDNAGREANA

The property developer P.V. Doyle built the houses next door to the Embassy, on the lands of Ardnagreana. This was his first venture into the property development business.

The house now has its entrance on Eaton Brae. The entrance was originally on Orwell Road. A school was run here by a Miss Barton from 1884 to 1900. The estate was developed in the 1950s to form Eaton Brae, and the house is now set in apartments.

Newtown House/Palermo has been demolished, and parts of Eaton Brae and Braemor Park were built on the lands of this estate. The name was changed to Newtown House around 1879, taking its name from the original Newtown House on Landscape Road, which was demolished in the 1850s. Werner, the well-known photographer, lived here.

ON THE OPPOSITE SIDE OF ORWELL ROAD

Sterling Park can still be seen at the end of the drive, a red-bricked house built in the 1870s by a vintner called Henry Crossley. He had his business at 8 Exchequer Street, and among its more interesting owners was Ed O'Keefe, a manure manufacturer of Blackpitts and Mill Street. I am not sure if he was a relation of the famous O'Keefe of the knacker's yard in the Liberties.

I can remember ponies being jumped here in the 1960s. At that time, if you had a few acres and a stable or two, the children always had ponies. Show jumping, gymkhanas and the Royal

Landore on Orwell Road, now hidden behind new houses.

Dublin Society events were hugely popular. Nearly all the local colleges and hospitals held annual gymkhanas up until the 1970s. The McGrane family were the last to live in Sterling Park before the lands were developed. It is now an exclusive avenue of stylish houses.

Landore House is still standing, tucked away behind the houses built on its land. The original estate extended all the way down to the Dodder river.

Michael Lyons, who owned Landore, was a paper merchant, and also had a printer's and stationer's business at 6 Ormond Quay. Lyons, being a Catholic, wanted his sons Patrick (aged thirteen) and John (aged ten) educated in the Catholic faith, and they were among the first half-dozen pupils registered at Terenure College when it opened in 1860.

In the grounds of Landore, on the left-hand wall at the top of the estate, is a bricked-up doorway. This was a connecting door between Landore and Geraldville, a house Lyons built for his daughter. The name was later changed to Beechmount. Just down Orwell Road, on the hill, is a bungalow with granite piers, which was the gate lodge of Geraldville. The newer houses, on the left coming up the hill, were built on the avenue of Beechmount.

ORWELL GARDENS

In the 1930s, the Dublin Commercial Public Utility Society was established. This commercial company built houses to rent, rather than to sell, in order to cater for couples who didn't have the money to purchase a house, but still needed a home. The estate was built on the lands of Landore.

ARCHBISHOP JOHN CHARLES MCQUAID

In the 1940s and 1950s, the Archbishop had a huge influence over Dublin, and in particular over the new parish of Churchtown. McQuaid (1895–1973), a Cavan man, had been a pupil at Blackrock College, and then entered the Holy Ghost Order, now called the Spiritans. Ordained in St Mary's College, Rathmines, in 1924, McQuaid became Dean of Studies in Blackrock College, then President of Blackrock in 1931. In 1940, he was consecrated Archbishop of Dublin. At the time, he was the only bishop from a religious order. This is significant. His actions were often individualistic and idiosyncratic, sometimes unsupported by the clergy of his dioceses. The bishops of Ireland did not always agree with his actions either.

Archbishop McQuaid established active Catholic social services, which did a lot of good work. The Archbishop had a strong relationship with the Taoiseach, Éamon de Valera, another past pupil of Blackrock College. McQuaid was consulted on the new constitution when it was being drafted in 1937, even though he was not Archbishop at the time. Father Denis Fahey of Blackrock College was another priest that de Valera consulted extensively. De Valera, in addition to being Taoiseach, was Minister of Education, and wanted certain policies ratified.

To this end, McQuaid was elected Chairman of the Catholic Headmasters Association. This association was the body with the most influence in the running of secondary schools in Ireland. McQuaid cultivated links in all places of influence, including in the planning departments of Dublin Corporation and Dublin County Council. A friend of mine, who worked in planning in Dublin County Council, recalled that when the Archbishop's car pulled up outside the offices,

The original Mount Carmel Hospital building, hidden away off the road.

they knew that 'for what he asked he would surely receive', through friendships with senior officials.

In the 1950s, Churchtown was one of several new and expanding parishes in Dublin. The Archbishop felt that the spiritual and educational needs of his people had to be catered for. He invited several religious orders into the area. He invited foreign orders of nuns, in particular the Little Company of Mary and the Notre Dames des Missions Sisters, and surprisingly ignored his own order, the Spiritans. He invited the De La Salle order to create schools in Churchtown.

Mount Carmel was originally named Ardavon. Joseph Hanley lived here until 1886, and then the Devine family, who were merchants in Little Britain Street, occupied the house until 1911. The Carmelites, who were running Terenure College at this time, set up a novitiate here, and changed the name to Mount Carmel.

The Little Company of Mary arrived at Mount Carmel on 19 September 1949, to establish a hospital. The Sisters were a nursing order founded in Hyson Green, England, by Mary Potter in 1877. The Mother House in Rome had been purchased with the help of George Noble Plunkett, father of Joseph Plunkett, one of the signatories of the 1916 Proclamation. The Pope granted George a papal knighthood because of this gesture. Thereafter he was known as Count Plunkett.

After visiting Rome in 1949, Archbishop McQuaid invited the nuns to open the hospital. The sisters of the Little Company of Mary were known as the 'blue nuns', due to the colour of their habit. While they were waiting for the renovations, the Sisters nursed patients in their own homes.

On 22 August 1950, the Archbishop officially opened the hospital, which was equipped to cater for thirty patients. The hospital gained a reputation for its maternity care. Many orders of nuns had initially experienced difficulty in obtaining permission from Rome to specialise in midwifery. It was regarded as unseemly work for single, celibate women.

Sister Brigid Canning, a member of the congregation, states, 'Many patients were apprehensive about having their confinements taken care of by religious sisters. Some felt they would not be given any pain-relieving drugs.' This notion was quickly dispelled, and Mount Carmel became a leading maternity hospital.

In 1960, the Archbishop opened the 'new' Mount Carmel, the original hospital becoming the sisters' convent. In the 1970s, the sisters once more extended the hospital, and set up a joint-replacement surgery unit there. A consultants' private clinic was opened in 1976.

The Church of Ireland Theological
College on Orwell Road.

MOBREEN©2019.

The family home of John Millington Synge at Newtown Villas, before they 'downsized' to number 4 Orwell Park.

The sisters sold the hospital to a property developer in 2002. The deal included the developer providing a purpose-built convent for the now ageing community. The hospital is now owned by the Health Service Executive, and is run as a nursing home for elderly patients.

The Church of Ireland Theological College was built by Miss Fetherstone Haugh, a philanthropic lady, originally as a convalescent home under the control of the Adelaide Hospital. Miss Featherstone Haugh was very particular about the ambient country setting in which she wanted her convalescent home located. The total cost was £6,416, which included £906 for railings and landscaping. It was opened in July 1894. It had enough room for twelve male and twelve female patients. It remained attached to the Adelaide Hospital until 1962, when the Church of Ireland Representative Body occupied it, and from then on it has been their theological college. Since then, all Church of Ireland ministers have studied here. The newer building on Braemor Park is the library, an endless source of valuable information.

BRAEMOR ROAD

Number 2 Newton Villas was the birthplace of John Millington Synge, on 16 April 1871. Synge did not spend long in this house, as his father died a year after his birth, and his mother moved the family to Orwell Park, next door to her mother.

Across the road is the park where the river called the Little Dargle flows. We also see Badger's Glen. There are still badgers here, and also a heronry in the trees. You can see the birds coming back each evening at dusk.

At the corner of Landscape Road and Braemor Road is the Glenside Pub, opened in 1954 by the builder James Brophy. He later built the Landscape cinema, just up the road from the pub. It opened on St Patrick's Day 1955, with the showing of *Three Coins in a Fountain*. The cinema seated around 900 people. Brophy ran into trouble with the trade unions, as he employed his untrained son as a projectionist. The cinema was closed in May 1957, and then re-opened in November 1958. When Teilifís Éireann started up in 1962, people tended to stay at home more, and the Landscape cinema finally closed in 1965. The last film shown was *Goldfinger*.

Newtown House stood on the right as you come up Braemor Road. The Redwood estate is built on its land, the giant redwood trees all that remains of the original magnificent gardens. *A Topographical Dictionary of Ireland* (1837) states that 'in the grounds … there are some very fine evergreens'.

Dr John Kirby lived here. Having gone to school in Lismore, County Waterford, he studied in Trinity College from 1802 to 1805. He then attended the Royal College of Surgeons of Ireland (RCSI), under professors William Dease and Abraham Colles. Much to their annoyance, in 1809, along with Dr Alexander Read, he founded the Theatre of Anatomy and School of Medicine. Initially in Stephen Street, it moved to Peter Street in 1810. The certificates from the school were accepted by all authorities, including the College of Surgeons of London and Edinburgh, but not by the RCSI, as his previous professors blocked him. The RCSI finally accepted his certificates in the 1820s. In 1832, he closed his medical school and became Chair of Medicine in the RSCI. He became President of the College in 1834.

When Kirby set up his School of Anatomy, it was a time of war in Europe. Many of his students went on to treat the wounded on the battlefields. This 1824 quote from *The Lancet* describes how he illustrated his lectures:

For the purpose of demonstrating the destructible effect of firearms upon the human frame, Bully's Acre (a pauper graveyard) gave up its cleverest treasures for the performance of the experiment. The subjects were placed with military precision along the wall, the lecturer entered with pistol in hand and levelling the mortiferous weapon at the enemy, magnanimously discharged several rounds each followed by repeated bursts of applause. As soon as the smoke and approbation subsided then came the tug-of-war. The wounded were examined, arteries were taken up, bullets were extracted, bones were set and every spectator fancied himself on the field of battle looking upon Mr Kirby as a prodigy of genius and valour for shooting dead men.

Kirby was a tireless worker, as shown in his autobiography:

From 1810 to 1814 my industry and labour were intense. I rose at five, at which hour I had a private pupil in my house, lectured him until seven, breakfasted, went to lecture to Peter St, classes till twelve, demonstrated at one, lectured at three, demonstrated at six, classes till ten.

In 1823, as President of the Royal College of Surgeons of Ireland, Dr Kirby bought the old Meath Hospital in the Coombe, which became the new Coombe maternity hospital. In 1839, he became the first consulting surgeon to the newly founded Adelaide hospital. His school of anatomy continued under various guises until 1889, when, known as the Ledwich, it was the last private school to be absorbed into the College of Surgeons.

26 Hillside Drive was the home of former Taoiseach Seán Lemass (1899–1971). Lemass has been called 'the father of modern Ireland'.

He was born in Capel Street, where his father was a hatter and outfitter. He went to school in Haddington Road and the Christian Brothers' school in North Richmond Street. Jimmy O'Dea, a famous comedian and panto star, was a schoolmate. Lemass joined the Irish Volunteers at the age of fifteen. At the age of sixteen, he was in the General Post Office during the 1916 Rising. He was arrested and taken to Richmond Barracks. After his release, he fought

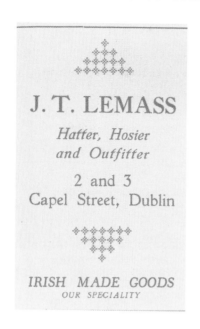

J. T. LEMASS

*Hatter, Hosier
and Outfitter*

2 and 3
Capel Street, Dublin

IRISH MADE GOODS
OUR SPECIALITY

An advertisement for the business of J.T. Lemass, father of
Taoiseach Seán Lemass.

in the War of Independence. In 1920, he was arrested again, and interred in Ballykinlar Camp, County Down. Although he was anti-Treaty, the Civil War deeply affected him for the rest of his life.

In 1926, Lemass was a founding member of Fianna Fáil. In 1932, he became Minister for Industry and Commerce, and during the Second World War, he was Minister for Supplies and Tánaiste. He became Taoiseach on 23 June 1959, succeeding Éamon de Valera. He was the first leader to move Ireland away from an insular viewpoint, looking towards Europe for the future of Ireland. He remained Taoiseach until 10 November 1966, and retired from the Dáil in 1969.

Seán Lemass didn't enjoy retirement long, as he died on 11 May 1971. He is buried in Dean's Grange Cemetery. He is still remembered as a man of great vision.

The Castle Golf Club is located at the end of Hillside Drive. It was founded in 1913 by builders Bailey and Gibson, who acquired the land from the Rathfarnham Demesne. The builders found it difficult to run the golf course, however, and a committee was formed to buy it from them. Its first President was Sir James Campbell (1851–1931). Campbell was educated at Trinity College, Dublin, and called to the bar in 1878, becoming a leading junior barrister, and eventually QC in 1892. He was a Unionist Member of Parliament from 1898 to 1916, during which time he became Solicitor General in 1903, and then Attorney General from 1905 until 1916.

A strong supporter of Edward Carson during the years of Home Rule agitation, he became a baron in 1917, taking the name Lord Glenavy of Milltown. He prosecuted Roger Casement and yet, later, after the establishment of the Free State, he became Chairman of the Senate. Although we had gained our freedom, Ireland clearly still needed establishment figures to help run the machinery of State. One of Campbell's grandsons was the well-known raconteur

Patrick Campbell. Lord Glenavy died in 1931, and is buried in Mount Jerome Cemetery, Harold's Cross.

Landscape Demesne was built by Sir George Ribton in the late 1770s. Sir George was a member of the Dublin Grand Jury, and a prominent figure in Dublin society. The family later moved from Landscape Demesne to Woodbrook House, near Bray. In a street ballad of 1868, his granddaughter, by all accounts a beautiful girl, was immortalised:

She charmed every gent she met
But I fear I shall fail in my duty
If I wedded an arrant coquette.

Landscape Manor was then occupied by the Quakers I referred to earlier – James Douglas and David Pedlow. In the twentieth century, Frank Ashby owned it.

Number 26 Hillside Drive, Churchtown, formerly the home of Sean Lemass, 1916 veteran, Taoiseach and great moderniser of Ireland.

When Archbishop McQuaid decided that he wanted to build a church in Churchtown, the first site he chose was Landscape Manor. Ashby found out that it was the Roman Catholics who wanted to buy the land, and he refused to sell. The De La Salle brothers, having been refused permission by the Archbishop to buy the house next to the Notre Dame School, then decided to purchase Landscape Manor. The brothers were cuter, and got a builder called Egan to buy Landscape Manor for them, so they were able to build their secondary school here in 1957. The cottages opposite the school were given to farm labourers in the early 1900s.

The Bottle Tower, the famous folly on Whitehall Road built in 1741 by Major Hall.

Rathfarnham Castle, a major landmark in the surrounding area.

WHITEHALL ROAD

This road gets its name from the Whitehall townland. There was also a house, now demolished, named Whitehall House. In 1742, the house was occupied by Major Hall, and to give employment, he constructed the folly now known as the Bottle Tower. Known originally as Hall's Barn, after the introduction of milk bottles the folly became known as the Bottle Tower. Note the dove cote beside it, a smaller version of the tower.

Hall's neighbour, in Rathfarnham Castle, was William Connolly (1662–1729), Speaker of the Irish Parliament from 1715 to 1729. He had built the famous Palladian mansion of Castletown House in Celbridge,

Two details from Ely Gate. Above right: One of the decorative urns that top the gate. Below right: A head, perhaps representing the spirit of the Dodder.

County Kildare. In the bad winter of 1742, his widow Katherine built a now-famous folly on the grounds of the estate, called Connolly's Wonderful Barn. Major Hall's folly is a miniature copy of Connolly's. Follies were often built to give employment to the destitute at the time. Money was rarely just handed out; it had to be earned.

Top: Berwick House on Whitehall Road, where working girls could take a break from their busy city lives. This was a residence of the De La Salle brothers, and ice cream makers Hughes Brothers ran their dairy farm here.
Left: Hazelbrook, now standing at Bunratty Folk Park.

Hughes Brothers' Hazelbrook Dairy provided 'Clean Milk for a Clean City', which is of course 'best for the bairns'.

Berwick House, built in 1740, was previously called Wax-field, Hazelbrook and Bachelors' Hall. In the early 1900s, a philanthropic lady called Miss Berwick, imbued with an evangelical spirit, opened this house to provide 'country air' to working girls from the city. Jacobs biscuit factory would give their more favoured employees a week in the country there. It existed for many years, until in 1944, the facility moved to Dalkey.

In 1953, the De La Salle brothers took over Berwick House, transferring their residence from Camberley House. The De La Salle brothers built their boys' national school on the grounds of the house. It opened in 1959, but because of declining numbers in the area, the school amalgamated with the Loreto Girls' National School in Rathfarnham, to form the Good Shepherd National School, which opened in 1989. This was the first parish school in Churchtown, established by Canon P.J. FitzSimons, with John Curran as Principal.

Hazelbrook was the base of Hughes Brothers, the ice cream makers. The Hughes brothers started farming in Berwick House in 1884. Then they built a house, which they named Hazelbrook, one of the original names of Berwick House. Hazelbrook was eventually transferred, brick by brick, to Bunratty Folk Park in County Clare in 2001.

In 1924, Hughes Brothers Dairy were the first in Ireland to pasteurise milk. The leading dairy in the city, they gave employment to hundreds around the area. Kieran Fagan gives a great account of the dairy in his book *The Story of HB* (2006). For years, their milk was delivered daily by horse and cart, which were eventually replaced by battery-operated floats. This system was clearly ahead of its time – now we're going back to battery-operated cars.

Hughes Brothers were taken over by Unilever, and the factory finally closed in August 2003. The buildings were all razed to the ground, and the large site is now being developed as a housing estate and apartments, under the name Hazelbrook Square.

Nutgrove Avenue

Nutgrove House, located near Rathfarnham, gave its name to the road. The gateway to the house had an inscription over it: 'Nutgrove Boarding School, established 1802'. The school was run by a Mr and Mrs Jones for many years, and it used to have a cricket team, which took on various teams around south County Dublin. William Domville Handcock went to school there. He wrote *The History and Antiquities of Tallaght* (1877). Nutgrove Boarding School was demolished in the 1870s.

Nutgrove Shopping Centre was built on the site of Holylands or Prospect Farm in 1800. In the mid-twentieth century, this was a fruit farm run by the Lamb brothers, another Quaker family. A lot of youngsters earned money during the summer picking fruit here. The old story went that the pickers got paid by the weight of the fruit, so to increase the weight, boys used to pee on the fruit!

The Lamb family also owned land near the Dodder, and donated some of it in the 1950s to build a Quaker meeting house. Situated in Crannagh Road, Rathfarnham Meeting House is still thriving.

The name Holylands came from the Mass path that led from the mountains to Booterstown Church. Holylands housing estate was built in 1960, though its name has since been changed to Mountain View.

The Church of the Good Shepherd was built as the church of ease of Rathfarnham Parish. In 1954, Dublin Corporation placed a compulsory purchase order on a parcel of land in order to build the Loreto Housing estate, then known as the Rathfarnham Housing Area. Archbishop McQuaid obtained some of this land to build his church. The first sod was cut in September 1954, and it was consecrated on 24 March 1957.

The names of all of the people who worked on building the church are in a milk bottle, buried in the porch. Just inside the gate is a plaque presented to the Parish by the Lemass family in 1991.

Father John (Jack) Thomas Hanlon (1913–68) was among the curates who worked here. Educated at Belvedere College and UCD, Father Hanlon was in the vanguard of Irish 'European' painters. Art was not taught in Belvedere, but under his mother's influence, Jack received private tuition. The family lived in Fortrose, Templeogue, and his father was a butcher with many shops around Dublin, including one at 107 Rathgar Road.

Hanlon became a pupil of Mainie Jellett, who introduced him to cubism. This had a major effect on him and cubism was reflected in his work for the rest of his life. His contemporaries included Evie Hone, Louis le Brocquy and Norah McGuinness. He exhibited at the Royal Hibernian Academy, in 1933 and 1938. He was ordained in 1939.

Hanlon was a founder member of the Irish Exhibition of Living Art, held in the National College of Art in Kildare Street in 1943. This exhibition is regarded as a watershed in painting in Ireland. He remained on the committee until his death in 1968.

In the *Irish Arts Review* (1988), John Coleman writes that 'he was a painter who owed much to the school of Paris and his mature works reflected a synthesis of Cubist and Fauvist influences fused with his very personal colour sense and subject matter.' He was one of the major first-generation modern Irish painters. Influenced greatly by French painters, he always used a light palette. 'I find Connemara and Donegal too sad and desolate,' he said.

The Church of the
Good Shepherd,
Churchtown,
consecrated in 1957.

The Church of the Good Shepherd under construction in the 1950s.

Father Hanlon was chosen to exhibit abroad on behalf of Ireland. He exhibited at the 1939 New York World Fair and competed in the Olympic Games art section in 1948. Indeed, the only medal Ireland won at those games was by his fellow artist Letitia Hamilton, who won bronze for her painting 'The Meath Hunt Point-to-Point Races'.

Father Hanlon inherited his sense of colour from his mother, who was a keen gardener. Father Hanlon was also a keen gardener, and in 1960, he won the novice section of the Horticultural Society's spring gardens competition.

In an interview published in *Ave Maria* (Notre Dame, Indiana), Father Hanlon stated that 'the primary purpose of all sacred art is to give an impetus to devotion … I like good abstract art … I would not like to produce it myself … I like realism but it must be interpretative realism.' Major religious commissions he undertook included work at the Navy Chapel, Haulbowline, County Cork; the chapel at Downings, Rosapenna, County Donegal; Saint Patrick's, Ardpatrick, County Limerick; Our Lady of Rosary Church, Ennis Road, Limerick; and Seaview Chapel, Ryde, Isle of Wight.

Hanlon was renowned in the parish for his intolerance for crying children, often stopping Mass to ask a highly embarrassed parent to remove a child from the church.

His artistic sensibilities are illustrated by a story told by a friend of mine, Seamus Kane. One Saturday evening, Kane's parents were walking by the church when his mother decided she must go to confession. Grabbing her husband's hat – a woman could not go into a church with her head uncovered – she went into the confessional. After Father Hanlon had given her absolution, he delayed her exit, saying, 'Madam, if I may give you some advice: I would change your milliner if I were you.'

Father Hanlon retired on 2 January 1967. The following year, he was taken ill in Tullamore, County Offaly, and was brought to Jervis Street Hospital, Dublin. But sadly he died on 12 August 1968, of a suspected burst appendix. In his will, he left his vast collection of paintings to various friends and galleries. Among his bequests, he gave an Evie Hone stained glass window to the Carmelite Fathers in Terenure. He is buried with his parents in Templeogue Cemetery, beside the Spawell Roundabout.

Canon Kenny was appointed the first parish priest of Churchtown in June 1965. He was succeeded in August 1981 by Father P.J. FitzSimons, who later became a canon. Canon FitzSimons was a great horse-racing man, whose claim to fame was that he was the last man to 'school' Mr What before that horse won the Grand National in 1958. In the event of his superiors finding out, he would have been severely reprimanded, if not defrocked.

The last parish priest was Father John Kileen, who was a keen photographer. The parish of the Good Shepherd, Churchtown, has now amalgamated with Rathfarnham Church again.

An unusual event that occurred in the Churchtown area was arranged by the Royal Dublin Society in August 1922. In its wisdom, the society decided to have a hackney car marathon. The race was eight miles long. It started at the Royal Dublin Society, then continued to Dundrum and up Churchtown Road Upper, then turned right onto Churchtown Road Lower, and then down to Milltown and back to the RDS. The Dublin Metropolitan Police patrolled the route, and excited crowds lined the roads.

The winner, Mr J. Murphy of 2 Albert Place, completed the course in forty minutes. This sounds like a pretty good time – five-minute miles. What a marvellous illustration of how rural the area was in 1922. Imagine the health and safety risk were it to happen now!

ACKNOWLEDGEMENTS

I am very grateful to all the people who have helped me write this book. Ideas, pictures, snippets of conversation, all were used. Special mention must go to a few people:

To my wife Dymps, who displayed endless patience and skill. Without whom this book would not have happened, nor would it have been worthwhile. Also thanks to our sons Mark and Barry for their technical knowledge.

To Vivien Igoe, whose enthusiasm, knowledge and editing skills helped me so much.

Thanks to the entire team at O'Brien Press, and in particular Eoin for his patience. A very special thanks must go to Michael O'Brien for his 'never say die' attitude, and whose wonderful illustrations have enhanced the book and made it special. Michael's quirky way of viewing things was so wonderful to see, particularly in the Churchtown area.

Thanks to Peter Pearson for his support and Foreword.

To my brothers and sisters for their continuing support and encouragement: many thanks Tony, Paul, Jackie and Irene.

I'm exceedingly grateful to the following people who have helped me along the way: Paul Barr, Alan Beasley, Nigel Bennett, Eddie Bohan, Angela Bourke, Geraldine Breen, Aidan Carr, Moira Cluskey, Jack Collins, Ronan Collins, Rodney Devitt, Paul Doolin, Carole Dunbar, Kieran Fagan, Edwin Finnegan, Tom Harris, Noel Healy, Jim Hegarty, Ger Henry, Fergal Kane, Seamus Kane, Ailbhe Kilvarry, Bernie Leavy, Niall Leinster, Mary Lumsden, Liz Meldon, Martin Morris, Mary Mc Aodha, Rev. J. Nolan, Angela O'Connell, Tom Ó Duinn, Declan O'Kelly, Ed O'Kelly, Seamus O'Maitiú, Peter Rossney, Gordan and Coral Ruddle, Christy Shanley, Terry Sheridan, Brian Sheahan, Kilian Walsh, David Waters, John Watters, Tommy, Kieran and Alison Webster.

I'd also like to acknowledge the support of some people who sadly are no longer with us: Michael and Eithne Colley, Paddy Conneff, Godfraí de Paor, Liam de Paor, Jo and Eugene Doolin, Robert Dunbar, Canon P.J. FitzSimons, Leo Healion, Padraig McGowan.

I want to thank the staff of the following institutions: the National Archives, the Gilbert Library, Religious Society of Friends library – particularly Glyn Douglas, Christ Church Presbyterian Church Rathgar – Edith Mayrs was of great assistance, the Irish Architectural Archives, R.I.A. archives and all the local libraries.

My thanks to all my friends in the Rathmines, Rathgar and Ranelagh local history society, the Old Dublin Society, the Local History Alumni Group and all at 112 Marlborough Street.

PICTURE CREDITS

Angela O'Connell, *The Servants' Church*: pages 12, 16 and 18; Declan O'Kelly: pages 22, 32, 33, 34, 35, 36 (all), 42, 47, 51 (top right) and 140; *The Irish Times*: page 30 (top); Christ Church Presbyterian Archives: pages 41 (all), 43 (top), 63 (right) and 89 (bottom); Peter Pearson: page 53 (right); Tony Farmer: page 68; Paddy Conneff: page 71; Vivien Igoe: pages 83, 84 and 122; *National University Handbook* 1908–1932: page 95; *Capuchin Annual*: page 102; Andrée Sheehy Skeffington, *Skeff*: page 103; *Republican Days: 75 years of Fianna Fáil*: page 121; *Thom's Directory*: page 127 (bottom); Nigel Bennett: page 142; Religious Society of Friends Archives: pages 147 and 151; Brian Sheahan: page 149; *Irish Arts Review* 1998 vol.14: page 162; David Waters: pages 168, 177, 183 (top left); Rodney Devitt: page 174; *Official Guide to Dublin*: page 193; Eugene Doolin: page 196 (all).

INDEX